The Glory Train

Glory Revival is Coming to the Nations!

Darren Canning

ENDORSEMENTS

I'm thrilled and excited to shout the news about the release of Darren Canning's new book, *The Glory Train*. This is no ordinary book. Its anointed revelation will make you hunger and thirst with an even greater yearning for the manifest presence of the Lord! Rejoice! Get excited because right now--today, the Glory Train of the Holy Spirit is visiting many cities and nations around the world, especially pouring out on those who are desperate to see the power of God released on the earth. In fact, I believe readers will be refreshed and infused with new passion, courage, and strength as they catch the vision of heaven! There's no more waiting because the time has come for what we've so long awaited--a time when His glory will fill both heaven and earth, and all men and nations will see and bow before the very King of kings and Lord of lords. We are living in an exciting time, so let *The Glory Train* rekindle the fire of your faith, as you read incredible testimonies that will bring this move of God to life--in a way that will leave you clamoring for more!

Steve Porter
Publisher/Deeper Life Press
Refuge Ministries

It's coming! God's amazing GLORY TRAIN is just around the bend. And for some of you, you've already hopped onto the train through God's acceleration in your life! In his newest book, THE GLORY TRAIN, Darren Canning's passion and excitement about the things God is showing him is certainly unquenchable. Read this "revelation from God's throne" and grab hold of the many specific directives from God and the new understandings HE is planting within our DNA of the days just ahead.

Two of my favorite chapters are, "The Coming 212 Revival – The Coming Of The Fire Of God" and "The Isaiah 54 Anointing: A Time To Expand And To Prosper!"

Grab your copy and get another copy for a friend! God is truly on the move with HIS GLORY TRAIN! —

Steve Shultz, Founder
THE ELIJAH LIST

A few years ago, God showed me a Vision of wild geese flying from Canada into the US. The early Celtic Christians called the Holy Spirit the wild goose because Holy Spirit is not a tame bird. Then He showed me younger men like Darren Canning carrying a "wild goose" anointing and God used them to help usher in the glory realm or the glory train. Darren's book is an invitation to escape the norm and jump aboard this powerful move of God. Can you hear it? It's on the way, gathering momentum in the Holy Spirit

Kathie Walters
Kathiewaltersministry.com

I love trains and I have always believed that they are a sign of God's favor and blessing to my ministry. For many years my meetings, around the world, have been interrupted by the sound of a train going by, often while we are receiving the offering! Trains are a symbol of provision and of ministries set loose by God for His purposes.

Those with eyes to see and ears to hear can't fail to see and hear the sounds of revival growing in many places on the earth. The Holy Spirit comes thru areas like a train and leaves a deposit of spiritual, financial and physical blessings that glorify God and expand the kingdom.

Darren Canning's new book, *The Glory Train*, expounds on what God is doing and reveals many insights into the means He is using to bring revival in our day. I heartily recommend that you study this book carefully and allow God to reveal to you what He expects from you. The Glory Train is for you! He wants you to experience that movement in all its power and grace. Get on board today.

Joan Hunter
Author/Healing Evangelist
Founder/President of Joan Hunter Ministries
Joan Hunter Ministries Canada

Everything that the Glory touches will change. The Glory of the Lord shall be visible in a greater dimension that we have ever seen before. Darren Canning's book "The Glory Train" is a valuable resource to the church in this hour. As you read this book I pray that you will be challenged to arise and shine and be a pursuer of His Presence a Glory carrier, for the Glory of the Lord is upon you and you shall see His Glory manifest in you and through you as you arise and shine.

Joe Garcia
The River International Church
www.theriverinyou.com

In reading The Glory Train, we could feel ourselves being pulled into the truth it contains. It was as if our spirit man was shouting, "Yes and amen!" In this book, Darren Canning has released a revelation of practical truth which has the ability to catapult you forward in advancing the Kingdom of Yahweh in the earth.

Mike and Susan Barnett
AS ONE United in Christ Fellowship Denham Springs, LA

There is something new brewing in the Spirit. Every time I go to Canada I feel the rumbling of a coming revival. The Lord spoke to me a few years ago that a fire of revival would start in Canada and spread to the nations. Darren Canning's book Glory Train will spark a fire and build your faith to go after all that God has for you!

Doug Addison
DougAddison.com
Prophetic author of Daily Prophetic Words and Spirit Connection webcast and blog

This is a generation that is crying out for genuine long-lasting revival. A generation of reformational revolutionaries that are pressing into heaven to see it released into the earth. "The Glory Train" is a book that will stir you to new realms of dreams and visions, activating your divine destiny and appetite for the miraculous, and leave you never being able to see your purpose on this earth the same. Get ready for the Glory Train to brand you and ignite you!

Nate Johnston
Everyday Revivalists

Darren Canning has an incredibly smooth, enjoyable writing style. Darren draws the reader into his stories, both exhorting and edifying the reader at the same time.
Darren has an intensely personal, experiential relationship with the God of the stories in his books. He knows God on a level for which most believers can only long. Darren encounters God in prophetic encounters, dreams, and visions, sharing those encounters with the reader. He has wisdom far beyond his years, wisdom that is only obtained by spending countless hours with God. Thankfully he shares that wisdom with us!
I have known Darren for several years. In that time, we have spent many

hours talking over coffee in my kitchen. He is the same person on the pages of his books, as he is in his conferences and meetings, as he is in my kitchen. He is a lover of God and a family man. He loves his wife, his children, and Jesus. He is the definition of "REAL"! He is a Glory Revivalist, and I am honored to know him.

May you be covered in glory dust as you enjoy this book!

Edie Bayer
Kingdom Promoters
www.KingdomPromoters.org
Author of *Power Thieves – 7 Spirits That Steal Your Power and How to Get It Back!; Write That Book! You Have a Book in You, Now Write It;* **and** *Narco, Awake O Sleeper*

I believe with all my heart that the next Great Move of God will be a Move of His Manifest Presence...His Glory! Now is the time that we need to aggressively be learning all we can about The Glory of God-- What is it? What effect does it have upon people? How can we move with it and facilitate it? What hinders the Glory?

I was attracted to my friend, Darren Canning, after I read an article he had written about the Glory. I said within myself, "There is a man who is after what I am after!" I sent him a copy of my book on the glory, "God Made Visible", and Darren read it. Soon, we met together in Canada and clicked instantly. What I like about Darren is his desire to go, "Out of the box', in his pursuit of God and His Glory! After he ministered at our church in Boulder, Colorado many came up to me and said, "Thank you for having that man! We appreciated his approach to ministry--nothing stuffy and religious! He was open and made himself vulnerable and approachable." Many are not willing to humble themselves like a little child and pursue God, and Humility is an indispensable key to attracting and stewarding the Glory of God! Are you willing to lay down your "Dignity?" Your professionalism? Your pre-conceived ideas of how God should always move? Then get ready to enter into Greater Glory!

I learned a great deal about the Glory from a British mentor, Arthur Burt, who was known for this prophecy that he called, "The Last Great Move of God."

"It shall come as a breath, and the breath shall bring the wind, and the wind shall bring the rain, and there shall be floods and floods and floods; and torrents and torrent and torrents! Souls shall be saved like leaves falling from mighty oaks swept by a hurricane. Arms and legs shall come down from Heaven, AND there shall be NO EBB."

People get ready! And may Darren's book be a great help and blessing to you along your way to Greater Glory!

Steve Shank
City on a Hill
Boulder, Colorado

Darren Canning is one of the most prolific End time prophetic Voices of our Generation, every Leader & believer alike need to not only read this book but listen to the sound of the glory train, coming in this Hour.

William Pollock
Joy Fire Ministry

The Glory Train is a timely book by my friend Darren Canning. There is presently a Psalms 107:9 generation on the scene that will settle for nothing less than the Spirit of God sweeping throughout the margins of society, birthed in the passionate hunger from His warrior bride in the earth. "For he satisfies the longing soul, and the hungry soul he fills with good things." Whet your appetite on amazing stories Darren shares combined with prophetic teaching and watch it leaving you thirsty for more and more! This is a good train and you should ride it!

Munday Martin
Founder of www.contagiousloveintl.com

"Darren Canning lives for revival. The dreams and visions he has received have caused him to believe for great outpourings of the Holy Spirit, bringing salvation and healing to masses of people. As you read this book, you too will be swept up into a passion to see the knowledge of the glory of the Lord cover the earth."

Wesley and Stacey Campbell
www.wesleyandstaceycampbell.com

In this day and age, we need the outpouring of the Holy Spirit more than ever. Darren is a prophetic revivalist that has been a friend to Field of Dreams Church. As you read this book I believe that your hunger will be stirred to partner with God to see heaven invade earth accompanied by dramatic supernatural manifestations.

Todd Weatherly
Founding Leader of Field of Dreams Church

FOREWORD

We are coming into a place in human history where all the deposits and anointing's from past generations will be poured out upon a Company of believers that have been prepared through a process to carry the Glory of God into nations with amazing proficiency, revelation, and power. This book *The Glory Train* by Darren Canning is a powerful tool to help you understand who you are and the call of God to bring revival power and revelation to this generation. Darren has amazingly knit together and articulated personal encounter with the word of God to unveil the strategy and heart of God to our generation.

Mantles in the Heavenly Locker Room

Several years ago, I was taken to a room in the Spirit that looked like a football locker room. In this room, I saw mantles hanging from shaker pegs and above the mantles were that names of great men and women of God in scripture and recent days that helped shape the course of history for breakthrough in their generation. I saw names like Elijah, Jeremiah, Enoch, Isaiah, Charles Finney, William Branham, Smith Wigglesworth, Maria Woodworth Etter, Katherine Kuhlman and others. The Lord was standing with me in this vision and said to me, *«Jeff, choose one, I'll give it to you».*

As I was pondering which mantle to choose I turned to the Lord and said, *«I don›t know which one to choose Lord, You choose for me".* Later in recalling this encounter to Bob Jones, he said, *«Boy that was the best answer you could have given the Lord, You let Him choose for you".* At that point, I found myself with a mortar and pestle in my hand and the Lord handed me three pills and said, *"Grind them".* As I was grinding the three pills the Lord said, *"These three pills are the past, present and future mantles that are being offered this generation".* The Lord was offering the cumulation of all past, present, and future mantles to be poured out upon a Glory generation that will be fully equipped to bring about the greatest revival and harvest the world has ever seen.

The Great Phoenix of the Holy Spirit

Recently I saw a great firebird in the Spirit flying over the city of Atlanta. The Firebird is commonly known as a Phoenix and Atlanta is known as the "Phoenix of the South". I watched as I saw the whole city set ablaze as the Holy Spirit flew crisscross over the city releasing a fresh baptism of the Holy Spirit upon those who were gathering and contending for outpouring and revival. I saw people coming out of wheelchairs, deaf were hearing and the blind saw, along with many staggering signs and wonders as the Fire Bird released wave after wave of fresh Holy Ghost power. The Lord was showing me that Atlanta was a prototype of what will happen in many cities globally. Immediately I thought of the Seraphim in Isaiah 6 that cried Holy, Holy, Holy, the whole earth is filled with His Glory.

In the year that King Uzziah died, I saw [in a vision] the Lord sitting on a throne, high and exalted, with the train of His royal robe filling the [most holy part of the] temple. 2 Above Him seraphim (heavenly beings) stood; each one had six wings: with two wings he covered his face, with two wings he covered his feet, and with two wings he flew. 3 And one called out to another, saying,

"Holy, Holy, Holy is the Lord of hosts;
The whole earth is filled with His glory."

4 And the foundations of the thresholds trembled at the voice of him who called out, and the temple was filling with smoke. Isaiah 6:1-4 AMP

Seraphim are "burning ones" that fly above the throne and the Lord of Glory. One of the functions of the Seraphim is "healing", Raphim (Jehovah Rapha - which is the God Who heals), so these burning ones that come out of the Presence of the Lord are literally burning, healing angels. This fiery Phoenix of the Spirit was being released over places of great hunger to release fresh miracles, healing, signs, and wonders to the sons of the Kingdom. We can begin to see healing revival burn in the most unexpected places in this new season.

Kingdom Family Business

All of these prophetic encounters and promises are wonderful but are pointing at something much greater. Yes, it's for revival, Yes it's for the harvest, but God has a much larger view in mind. We can describe the plan of God as simple. It is to extend the rule of His unseen Kingdom through a family of heirs—sons and daughters. These offspring will act as God, on behalf of God, being His legal representatives and judiciaries on the planet, carrying out His orders and implementing the will of their Father and older heavenly Brother, Jesus Christ. From the dawn of time it has always been about family—about the Father and His children—and it will continue to be so until the end days. It's high time now for us to be about the Father's business. After the resurrection, Jesus told Mary, who was the first to see Him,

Go to My brothers and say to them, I'm ascending to My Father and your Father, and to My God and your God. (John 20: 17 NKJV).

We are the brothers and sisters of Jesus. His Father is our Father; His God is our God. Jesus is the firstborn among many brothers:

"For God knew His people in advance, and He chose them to become like His Son, so that His Son would be the first-born among many brothers and sisters" (Rom. 8: 29 NLT).

Jesus is the prototype for all His brothers and sisters who find their way to the Father to share with Him as heirs of the coming Kingdom. Jesus was not ashamed to call us brothers because we are family with Him.

"As many as received Him, to them He gave the right to become children of God, even to those who believe in His name" (John 1: 12).

He gave those who believe in His name the right, ability, and privilege to become children of God.

A New Place in Human History

We are in a place and time in human history where we are starting to see the children of the Kingdom come into maturity. These seeds are coming of age and are beginning to bringing about fruit that resembles the original Seed, Jesus Christ. Through His children, God is establishing His Kingdom and purposes on the earth. He rules the seen world from the unseen world through our spirit and is birthing His initiatives through us in the physical world. The fruitful journey of Jesus was well documented as He traveled about cities and villages, teaching in their synagogues, proclaiming the good news, the Gospel of the Kingdom of God. He cured every sickness, disease, and infirmity that He encountered, further preparing the soil and sowing the precious seed (see Matt. 4: 23; 9: 35). Everywhere He preached the gospel, Jesus displayed His power with wild miracles, signs, and wonders. God expects His family to do the same thing—acting the same way as Jesus did. Because you are sons, God has sent the Spirit of His Son into our hearts, crying, "Abba! Father!" Romans 8.

Therefore you are no longer a slave, but a son; and if a son, then an heir through God (Galatians 4: 6-7).

Adam's rebellion toward God ended in spiritual death, resulting in separation from God. But now what was hidden deep in the spirit of man is being uncovered and rediscovered by a family of sons and daughters of God all around the world. All things have been put in subjection under the feet of Jesus Christ and we are part of His Body—so all things are under our feet.

In Conclusion - The Lion of Judah is Roaring Again

It took the death of Jesus Christ, the One True Heavenly King, to restore us to our rightful place as kings and lords of the earth. It was for the joy that was set before Him that He endured the cross, knowing that on the other side of the pain there would be you and I, the redeemed sons and daughters of the Heavenly King. His intention was that the one true Heavenly King (Jesus) would live through the many kings on the earth and establish His reign of authority through a family. So, in this final chapter of human history and on this side of eternity, the Lion of the Tribe of Judah is roaring again

The final chapter of these events will be so terrible, so incredible in the earth that even the elements will shudder with great shaking as angels and demons wage war in the heavenly realm. Intercession will focus on the arrival and coming forth of a Kingdom family who is filled with the sound of His roar. They will have power and authority to manifest the glory of God in the earth, breaking the curse over creation and releasing healing in the nations, causing them to flourish once again in the glorious freedom for which they were created. Some would say, Jeff, this is too far-reaching, merely visions of grandeur! In reality, these scriptural truths are yet to be apprehended and walked out by a supernatural Church—the called out ones or the ecclesia. This company of believers will reach far beyond the normative mind-sets of the day and demonstrate the miraculous in ways not seen in Church history. Jesus Christ paid the ultimate price in blood through Calvary to open the heavens and restore to us the keys to the Kingdom. He will reap the reward of His suffering.

Even now, the clash between heaven and earth is mounting. Darkness has become increasingly dark and powerful as we draw near to the end and toward the Great Revival. The Church is under pressure and is being squeezed to produce the sweet wine of heaven. There are great pressures in the earth and pressure in the heavens. Cosmic violence is beginning to spill out upon the earth. Heaven is not for the faint of heart but is a violent realm causing even the strongest to fear and tremble. This heavenly fury will be poured out in these last days upon an end-time army of God that has been prepared to carry it. And this army will unleash the Spirit of Revival in the nations of the earth. We must get ready for the unleashing of the furious sound of glory—the roar of power and love that transforms the earth. (Excerpt from Furious Sound of Glory - Jeff Jansen)

As you read *The Glory Train* you will begin to see a picture and the price Jesus paid for you to look and act just like Him. God is pouring out His spirit in a fresh new way and this amazing book by Darren Canning will help you get the keys to understanding your role and place in the greatest outpouring of Gods Spirit the earth will ever see. Get ready, The Glory Train is coming to a city near you.

Jeff Jansen
Global Fire Ministries International
Senior Leader Global Fire Church and Global Connect
Founder of Global Fire Ministries International
Author of Glory Rising & Furious Sound of Glory
www.globalfireministries.com

INTRODUCTION— THE GLORY TRAIN

I am not sure when I first heard of the Glory Train, but it has always represented revival to me. I have actually seen the train in visions and dreams many times. Years ago, I was a part of a revival in Ottawa Valley. One night, I saw the glory train in my dream. It was winding its way through the valley and glory was being released wherever it went. That revival touched thousands in the valley. Many healings took place and many were prophesied over. People's lives were shifted into the blessings of the Lord.

Kathie Walters is a close friend of mine. Many years ago, she came to my region. I was so new to all the manifestations of the presence. I had no idea of the things I would see in the years ahead. She told me that she saw me being given a glory tie. From that day till now, I have seen thousands of miracles in meetings.

To me, the glory is the presence of God. As we honor Him and make Him front and center in our lives, His presence comes strongly. In the Glory is everything I need and that is mostly the character of God's heart resting on my own. In His presence is fullness of joy (Psalm 16:11) and His peace that transcends understanding (Philippians 4:7). When these come fully in my heart, I am in the shelter of the Most High. It is the place of safety from every earthly storm.

I have traveled to many nations and will travel to many more. Everywhere I go, the presence of God invades atmospheres and changes people's lives. I have seen the glory invade rooms and healings have come. I have seen angels manifest, bringing fire and deliverance. I have seen oil miracles and gold miracles and gemstone miracles. I have seen rainfall in rooms and I have seen even more unique things.

This used to scare me because people started calling me a false prophet when the miracles began. I had to learn to preach the name of Jesus like I had never done before. In every meeting, I declare that miracles, signs, and wonders follow the preaching of the gospel, and the gospel is that Jesus came and died and rose again so that you and I would not have to remain in the torment of the old nature.

The first miracle that Jesus performed was turning water into wine (John 2:1-11). This was a prophetic act which I believe represented what Jesus came to do on Earth. He transformed dirty water from ceremonial cleansing pots into what was considered the best wine. This was a prophetic description of the miracles Jesus performs within every believer that turns to him. His glory comes and transforms them from the old nature into the new – all by the grace of God.

The glory train is a release of heaven's atmosphere into Earth. In this collision comes the most beautiful array of glory. People are shifted from glory to glory and strength to strength. They are made new and begin to journey deeper into truth and deeper into the destinies that God has for their lives. They become carriers of His presence.

You and I change the world when the glory of God manifests through our lives. In Christ, you become part of the glory train. Out of your inner man flows rivers of living water (John 7:38) and wherever you go, people's lives will be shifted from the old into the new, by no power of your own, but by the power of Jesus Christ living within you.

You will receive power when the Holy Spirit comes on you (Acts 1:8). For the Holy Spirit lives with you and will be in you (John 14:17). When you accept this by faith and operate in it from a place of certainty, many signs and wonders will follow your life. You will not hesitate to believe because everywhere you have gone it has happened, so it will continue to happen everywhere you will go.

Imagine now and believe in your heart that there is a mighty army of people rising with the certainty in their heart that they are victorious in Christ Jesus and that things will shift and change everywhere they go. If you see it then you are seeing what is about to happen on Earth. God is doing it. You can be a part of that train. God will use you to do great things.

I pray that as you read this book, you will be inspired to believe in greater things. I pray that you will have your eyes opened to see the power of Christ within you. Did you know that the same Spirit that raised Christ from the dead abides in you? You are a tabernacle or resting place of the Holy Spirit. He is just waiting for your belief to be activated for great things.

This is the season, the beginning of a great wave of glory being released on Earth. I declare you will ride that wave.

Blessings to you,

Darren Canning
July 1, 2017

TABLE OF CONTENTS

CHAPTER 1

THE COMING RAINS OF REVIVAL

Revival Waves

Over the last number of months, I have had dreams that speak to me about the hour we are now entering.

I had a recent vision while waking up of a floodgate on a river's dam. It lifted and the waters began to rush out quickly. I was standing in the river as the floodgate opened and watched as the water rose fast to my knees. It was like a torrent and I was a little nervous that it might knock me down, but I kept standing and watching.

Then I had another dream. I was standing at the edge of a great ocean. I was a couple of hundred feet above it, in fact. I was standing next to a man who told me about how a great wave had just come to shore which no one expected. I was standing next to a house in this dream and the man was standing near a sand dune 30 feet past the house. I then saw him as he must have been when the wave struck. I saw the shock on his face and how he was thrown back.

I sense that we have entered into a new season in the Church. I believe revival is rising among us. We are sensing an increase in the presence of the Holy Spirit in our meetings, and I have been hearing reports from my friends who are testifying to a "heightened anointing" in their meetings. An increasing number of people seem to be touched, and miracles and healings are happening more often and with greater impact.

I was ministering in Canada recently at a church that was located in a garage. We had a move of the Spirit there. A man and a woman with their six children were present from the Old Order Mennonite faith. They had gold appear on them in that meeting. Well, they went back home and the very next week, gold began to break out on their children. Then it started showing up at their house church on Wednesday night. They told me just recently that deliverance and healings are taking place as people come under the presence of the Lord. This has been happening for two months. They are seeing *Isaiah 60:2* take place in their midst:

"For behold, the darkness shall cover the earth, and deep darkness the people; But the Lord will arise over you, and His glory will be seen upon you."

Dreams and Visions Are Rising

The waters of vision are rising. I sense that many will enter into a place of dreams and visions granted by the Holy Spirit. We are going to see the fulfillment of *Acts 2:17* in our times: ***"'And it shall come to pass in the last days,'***

says God, 'That I will pour out of My Spirit on all flesh; Your sons and your daughters shall prophesy, Your young men shall see visions, Your old men shall dream dreams.'" Many are about to testify to the wild dreams they are being given by God.

This is the hour of *Ezekiel 47:4: "He measured off another thousand cubits and led me through water that was knee-deep. He measured off another thousand and led me through water that was up to the waist."* The angels have come and they are leading us into the waters of greater revival.

Two years ago, I had a dream with Bob Jones in it. In this dream, Bob and I were driving through Toronto on Highway 401, one of the largest freeways in North America. Bob was driving very slowly. He looked over at me and said, "Explosions, explosions, explosions."

I had the privilege of asking Bob about this dream in the Fall of 2012 in New Bern, North Carolina. I remember he got very excited when he heard me speak of my dream. He told when he was in his 60s, he prophesied revival would come to Toronto. He said that he had prophesied the Toronto Blessing Outpouring, even naming John Arnott as the person God would use as a part of that great work.

But, he said, "Toronto represented an ankle-deep revival, and there were greater revivals coming to Canada." He said that one revival would bring us to our knees and the other would bring us over our head. 1994 represented one explosion, but he told me to expect others and even greater ones.

In those meetings with Bob, many prophesied of a coming wave. I have been hearing about this wave for many years. I have seen it in dreams and visions for the last 10 years. It will come upon the Church and the people will be suddenly touched by the power of God. Many will not expect or even desire what God is about to do, but they will be touched and swallowed up by it nonetheless.

He mentioned that, as this occurred in Canada, it would also begin to pour out into the United States. In fact, I have seen God perform tremendous miracles, signs, and wonders in that wonderful nation. God is not done with the USA, as some might suppose. I believe that the greatest days for the USA are about to arrive.

Rain and Thunder

Another thing I have been hearing in this season is *Isaiah 44:1-4L* *"'Yet hear now, O Jacob My servant, and Israel whom I have chosen.' Thus says the Lord who made you and formed you from the womb, who will help you: 'Fear not, O Jacob My servant; And you, Jeshurun, whom I have chosen. For I will pour water on him who is thirsty, and floods on the dry ground; I will pour My Spirit on your descendants, And My blessing on your offspring; They will spring up among the grass like willows by the watercourses.'"*

God is pouring out His Spirit on dry ground. I started hearing this two years ago and everywhere I go proclaiming this

Scripture, I see incredible rain and thunderstorms take place – **in Kansas, Texas, New York State, Pennsylvania, New Jersey and in Canada.**

I went to Texas sometime last year and decided to bring my rain jacket because of all the rain I was experiencing. Well, the people in Texas thought I was funny because they had not been experiencing much rain for two months. I told them it would rain, and rain it did. It rained so hard that the leaders were thanking the people on the second night for facing the bad weather to make it to the meeting. It was easy to minister that night because there was such an expectation that God's glory would be poured out.

In Canada last summer, we had three days of meetings. The thunder was so strong it kept knocking the sound system out. One minister at that meeting, Mark Redner, prayed for people past midnight. Over 60 people were healed, some from conditions they had for 20 years. Mark went back into that region two or three months later and revival broke out in Waterloo lasting three weeks. Close to 500 people came each night, and many were healed of all kinds of conditions. People were being pulled out of wheelchairs.

In San Antonio two months ago, we ministered at a little church where the preacher told me she wanted to close the church down because the work just didn't seem to be moving ahead. Today, about eight weeks later, that church has been in revival for about 30 days straight. Hundreds of people have come there to experience the refreshing that is taking place through worship and the preaching of the Word.

<u>The Great Wave and Outpouring</u>

God is on the move and those who are thirsty shall be filled. *John 7:37-38* says, ***"On the last day, that great day of the feast, Jesus stood and cried out, saying, 'If anyone thirsts, let him come to Me and drink. He who believes in Me, as the Scripture has said, out of his heart will flow rivers of living water.'"***

I believe we are entering the season of the great wave and the great outpouring. The floodgates to the river are being lifted up and many will drink of its waters. The heavens are about to burst with rains falling on thirsty hearts. Get ready for a greater depth of the Holy Spirit in our hearts. He is coming, riding on the waves. He is the Helper, the Sanctifier, and He is coming to clean up the church. He is going to reveal the coming King.

If you are reading this, I believe it is your challenge to step into the river of revival. I believe that God is about to visit North America in an unprecedented way. Open your hearts and let the waters come. Call out to God like the blind man demanding He does not pass you by. You will be filled to overflowing and out of you will flow rivers of water that bring salvation and healing to all nations.

CHAPTER 2

A VISION OF A SPIRITUAL ROCKET – TIME FOR TAKE OFF!

As we approached the end of the year 2015 under the Gregorian calendar and near the beginning of the year 5775 under the Biblical calendar, I had a few insights about the coming season.

I have heard many people speak about "a rocket that is about to take off in the spirit" over the last number of months. For me personally, this word has deep meaning. It has been spoken over my life by four to five prophetic people and I have seen it in dreams, so I believe that I am about to experience a wild acceleration in my life and ministry in the coming season, certainly as we cross into 2018.

But, I have also come to look at my life as a prophetic statement for the Body of Christ. The prophet's life is often like this, and so I am certain that what God is doing in my life, He is about to do in the lives of many others in the Body at the same time.

<u>The Ignition Switch is Being Lit</u>

There are some reading this right now who are about to cross into new plains of life. I believe that personal ministries, careers, artistic expressions (writing, arts, and photography, etc.) are about to begin. I believe that this also applies to social media ministries. Some people that are about to be filled with strategies to reach even more people for Christ through this medium.

Get ready! God is about to light the ignition and you are about to take off into realms that you have not been in before.

As I was considering this word, I came across an article about NASA's new space program, the Orion Rocket. This month will begin a new phase for NASA. They are initiating a new space program with the hope of developing technology for deep space flight. Humans have not traveled this far since 1972.

That this is happening now, when all of these rocket words are coming forth, seems to suggest to me that this is bigger than you or me. I believe that a great revelation is about to come from God to mankind. I also believe that the revelation is going to bring us to deeper places in the spirit that have not been seen in a long time – at least in this generation.

<u>Economic Acceleration</u>

Moreover, we are in a time of economic acceleration brought on in part by the downward trend in gasoline prices. This is a phenomenon that has positive outcomes for most of the world's economies. There is currently an acceleration taking place in the natural world because of this positive externality. There are positive outcomes occurring for every family because of cheaper gas.

So I believe there is benefit coming to many in the Body of Christ in 2017. As we cross over the threshold into the New Year, you should expect to take off in your lives and expect God to begin to end some of the struggles you have been going through. You will receive revelation and strategy on how to proceed. You will also be propelled into the next level for your lives and career.

CHAPTER 3

THE GOLDEN SLIPPERS ANOINTING: NEW SHOES FOR NEW MINISTRIES

This is the hour of the golden slippers. This is the hour that you have been crying and groaning for. **This is the season when God is handing out shoes for new ministries**. They shall come forth in many numbers. Many shall rise and wander into the highways and byways, converting the masses to the heart of Christ. This is the hour that the ancient Christians groaned for. They saw it during their time.

This is the hour of finances being released for Kingdom assignments. Bags of gold will be laid at your feet. You will walk and not grow weary, run and not faint. A thousand may fall at your side and ten thousand at your other side, but you will leap like a calf from its stall and enter into the glory of God.

Angels are being assigned to walk with you and these will release the miracles, signs, and wonders in the

atmospheres of the rooms you will enter. Get ready: this is the moment you have been longing for.

Hunger and Anointing Increasing

Recently, I ministered in Hamilton, Kitchener, and Toronto. Everywhere we went we saw people longing for the presence of God. One man was so hungry for more of God that he held my hand and looked into my eyes for 10 minutes. I gave him the bandana I was wearing on my head and he slept with it all night because he wanted to have dreams of angels. **That is childlike hunger and that is the heart of the Army rising in the earth at this time. They will not care what others think because they long for the anointing of God.**

I remember I saw an angel in a dream a number of months ago. He was a craftsman and had great skill in creating gemstones. Each stone he created was amazing in color and detail. I knew an hour was coming when these would be released into the atmosphere. Some were small and others were very big. Each stone released will speak prophetically in the moment that it's released. Two of these stones appeared in our midst in Hamilton in February.

I saw a piece of heavenly glass that looked like a woman's foot in a Golden Slipper. This miracle is why I am prophesying the way I am today. **I felt that this was a sign that God is releasing a tremendous anointing to His servants starting even now.**

I did a little research to see if there was anything interesting about the golden slipper in Christian lore, and there was indeed something very interesting. In 1879, an African-American man by the name of James A. Bland wrote a hymn called "Dem Golden Slippers." There is a line in the song that says, "Golden slippers I goin' to wear to walk the golden street." Another interesting coincidence is that there is a version of the hymn on YouTube by the Fisk University Jubilee Quartet from 1909, which just happens to be during the Azusa Street Revival years.

Do you think perhaps God is saying something here? **I believe we are entering into a greater revival even in this hour. Get ready!**

We also saw a diamond-like stone in Hamilton. I gave it to a lady after I picked it up, but when she got up to preach, she accidentally threw it into the air, which really is a prophetic act all on its own. Get ready for the warriors to arise and fly with eagle's wings into unknown places.

After these meetings in Hamilton, we went to Kitchener and crazy signs and wonders happened there as well. There was an angel in that meeting releasing aromas into the atmosphere. There were only about 45 people in the room but I believe that most of them smelled something. There was the smell of cotton candy (childlike faith), Rose of Sharon (healing presence of Jesus), cake (party in the spirit with the Word), mint (refreshing), and bread (the presence of Jesus as the Word of God). Also, glory dust appeared on many people. Many colors too: greens, oranges, reds, yellow gold, and silver; and all of this is a sign of the coming glory of God being released to the masses.

<u>Say, "God, I Am Available!"</u>

God is awakening hearts in this hour. All you have to do is step in and say, "God, I am available." You will enter if you are hungry.

A golden slipper reminds me of the story of Cinderella. In order to go from the rags of humanity to the riches of the Kingdom, it will take childlike faith. You will not receive your slippers until you rejoice and enter into the things that God is doing by faith. You will experience many things, but you have to allow God to open your heart.

It starts with one declaration: "Lord, no matter what You do, I will enter into Your presence as long as it is You. So convince me, Lord."

CHAPTER 4

RAPID INCREASE! HEALERS, PROPHETS, DREAM INTERPRETERS, SEERS RECEIVING A DOUBLE PORTION

Rapid Increase For Those New in Christ

In a recent dream, I saw that there is a new anointing rising in the earth at this hour in order to bring in the harvest. God is about to teach people to walk in the gifts of the Spirit at a very rapid pace. I see people who are "new to Christ" learning to fly in the things of the spirit quickly, because they will be aligned to Godly mentors who will teach them quickly.

This will be like on-the-job training in the things of the spirit learning to operate in supernatural ways. God is going to bypass the normal learning cycle and even train people through dreams and visions.

This is the hour of Ezekiel 37 when the army of God is being resurrected from dry dead bones. Those that are about to rise in the army are not even aware that the army exists but arise they will into greater destiny than they ever imagined possible.

Let Them Join Our Flight

I saw in this dream that there was a young person that started to fly alongside of me. I was moving very quickly in the spirit, flying from city to city. I was operating by faith as I flew between cities. The person next to me said that the gate to the city is not opened, so you will need to slow down, but in the spirit, I knew we didn't have to slow down because the gate would open as we got near to it.

We were flying side-by-side, and as we came to the city a glass door opened before us and we flew quickly into that city. We then began to operate in the gifts of the Holy Spirit in a way that I personally had not operated before. There was a young lady in that dream who was an aspiring actress. Because of disappointment she was not actually acting. She was living below her potential because depression came against her. She was far from Christ and banqueting at the world's table.

In my heart, I was trying to get to as many people as I could in order to get the message of Christ to them. This young girl and those sitting with her, mocked the message of Christ when I approached them; but then I began to tell her things that only she and God knew, and as I did something shifted in her mindset. I told her that she would have been in the movies now if she had listened to the advice that one director had given to her a while back. She looked at me shocked and then began to listen to the message of Christ that we preached.

The person flying with me was learning as we walked together. I know that in this hour that many of us who have been in the things of the spirit for some time will be taking responsibility for training those that are young in the things of the spirit, but these ones will actually learn to fly by being with us. Those of us who have exercised our faith will have many people who will want to learn from us and we must let them join us in our flights.

We don't have to slow down for them. We don't even have to worry about them. They will keep up with us because the Holy Spirit is guiding them to us and teaching them to fly like us. All we have to do is **be open to the possibility that God has them coming to us, and when they do just let them hang out and ask questions. There will be an impartation in the process of mentoring.**

They will learn to fly in the same way we do. They will also have gifting that we don't have and will teach us a thing or two. God is uniting the army in this hour. **Get ready for expansion on your left and right.**

Expansion and Giant Steps For the Kingdom

Isaiah 54:2-3 says, "**Enlarge the place of your tent, stretch your tent curtains wide, do not hold back; lengthen your cords, strengthen your stakes. For you will spread out to**

the right and to the left; your descendants will dispossess nations and settle in their desolate cities."

This is what the Lord is saying: **Those of you who have ears to hear listen to what the Spirit is saying. Do not fear the finances, do not fear rejection, do not fear fear itself, because you are about to take giant steps for the Kingdom sake.**

A few weeks ago I had another dream. **This is a season where people are being upgraded into new anointings and mantles.** Even with the passing of men and women who have gone before us, there is a transfer taking place between generations. People in their 20s and 30s are about to take their place in the Kingdom.

God is taking your old shoes and releasing new shoes in this hour. People will notice the increase of anointing upon your life. There will be an increase in the healing and prophetic anointing. You will walk in it with greater ease.

The Lord showed me in that vision that He is releasing many spiritual blessings over those who are ready to be raised to the next level. This new season will be very exciting for those in-tune with the things of the Holy Spirit. Get ready for a double portion. Even as Elisha received a double portion of Elijah's anointing (*2 Kings 2:9-16*), **the next generation of healers, prophets, dream interpreters, and seers are receiving a double portion.**

You will move like Philip did, releasing the good news to

many places (*Acts 8:39*). You will be like the man from Macedonia who showed up in Paul's dream to tell him to come preach the Gospel in Macedonia (*Acts 16:9*). God is going to do this by His Spirit.

Isaiah 44:3-4: "**For I will pour water on the thirsty land, and streams on the dry ground; I will pour out My Spirit on your offspring, and My blessing on your descendants. They will spring up like grass in a meadow, like poplar trees by flowing streams.**"

Seek the greater gifts and you shall walk in them. Get ready for a new dimension of glory. Get ready for a new shift.

Even as we move between seasons in the natural we will be moving between seasons in the spirit. Watch for what occurs in the next number of months. With the abundant rains of spring will come a new thing in the earth in this hour.

CHAPTER 5

THE BEGINNINGS OF A GREAT MOVE – AMONGST PRESENT DARKNESS

I was reading about St. Brendan a couple of days ago. He was a Monk who was born in the amazing era when Christianity was being introduced to Ireland in the fifth and sixth centuries AD. What really intrigued me about him was his desire to reach the nations around him for the Lord.

St. Brendan started many monasteries in Ireland and even in far-off places in his time like Scotland. He was an apostolic father who gathered others around him to affect nations for the Lord. **I am sensing that what was on his life is about to rise upon the lives of some men and women of God in our time.**

I guess because I come from the island of Newfoundland in Canada, I am intrigued by people who once sailed the big, wide oceans for adventure and missionary assignments before the modern era. In fact, some of my own family crossed that wild ocean from England to Newfoundland to do missionary work.

The faith of these people amazes me because I have seen how big the waves in Newfoundland can get. The North Atlantic is not a water that you want to find yourself in. Even in the summer, the waters are very cold and dark, but the bluest blues you can imagine. So when St. Brendan set sail from Ireland to do exploits in similar waters for the Lord, this was a voyage of great faith but he trusted God and as a result saw God do wonderful things.

The Beginnings of a Great Move

It takes great faith to do great things for God. I really believe that we are on the cusp of the greatest revival the earth has ever seen. Even now many nations are feeling the beginnings of a great move of the Spirit. I was recently in New Zealand and Australia. We ministered to almost 800 people in 10 days. I prophesied over 400 or 500 people myself. God touched those hearts deeply. I could sense the presence of God in a most special way.

While in Melbourne, I had the opportunity to go to the birthplace of the Pentecostal movement in Australia. It was started by an amazing woman named Janet Lancaster in a building on Russell Street. The name of the work was the Good News Hall. It was started in 1909. For those of you who know your history that was during the years of Azusa Street revival in Los Angeles. Many well-known ministers of the early Pentecostal movement went to this place in Melbourne to speak including Aimee Semple McPherson and Smith Wigglesworth.

In fact, the day that we visited this historic revival site would have been Smith's 156th birthday. When he preached in Melbourne there was a tremendous move of the Holy Spirit. They say that over 2000 people were filled with the Holy Spirit with the evidence of speaking in tongues.

It was prophetic that we were there on his birthday. **I sense that God is releasing a new anointing in this hour. What was on the lives of the great saints of past generations, including those like St. Brendan of Ireland and the Wigglesworth, is about to come forth and be birthed again in the new generation.**

One of the visions I had in Australia, in particular, was of a young woman who grew eagle's wings. I saw this in a trance. It was as if I was standing right next to this young lady. I felt that this was a particular word for Australia, but have since considered that this was something that God is doing in this hour among women worldwide.

Women and The Next Generation of Seers and Prophetic Voices

God is going to raise up the young ladies of the next generation to become powerful seers and prophetic voices to their generations. They are going to see in very accurate ways. They are going to be a part of a legion of young women who will rise to see their cities taken for the Lord.

In fact, while in Adelaide, I went into a Museum and saw pictures of women who served in World War I as nurses. There was an amazing picture of hundreds of women dressed in white nursing uniforms marching through the streets. They were excited to serve the men who were being hurt by war. They did not fear for their lives but were content to serve their nation in the way they were being called to do so.

That same zeal is reawakening in the earth in this hour. I can see a mighty wave of women rising into their destinies. God is going to use those who say, "I will." On that trip to Australia, I met some young women that exemplified this word. I was amazed at the zeal and passion for the Lord in their lives.

Not only are the women going to be touched but the men will as well. I see a new anointing that is about to emerge upon the people of my era. I see them being inspired by the Holy Spirit to step out in a new way. They are going to be forerunners that are going to usher in a new era of world-wide missions. They will not fear their lives even unto death. Even in the hour when ISIS is on the rise these ones will look into the face of this present darkness and command it to cease and desist.

A Dream of ISIS and Present Darkness

In fact, recently I had a dream. I saw, if you will, a very dark place where people were given over to worshipping the evil one. I was sitting in the room with them. I was uncomfortable being there in the dream but soon realized God had me there on assignment.

There was a woman there who had a very serious problem with her back. It may have been Scoliosis. I began to command her back to be healed and when I did, there was a cracking and she stood right up. Before the healing, she was completely hunched over sitting in a wheelchair. When this healing took place she jumped up rejoicing in what God had done.

As you can imagine I was very excited, but then I was standing at the top of a set of stairs leading into the basement. I heard a commotion down there and suddenly a spirit ran up to speak to me. This was the spirit of ISIS.

It said to me, "Because you are involved in these healings I am sending out my ISIS fighters and they are about to kill Christians worldwide." I looked at him and an authority rose up in my heart. I said, **"No, that is not what is about to happen. In fact, your ISIS fighters are about to come to Jesus Christ as their Lord and Savior."** When I said this there was like an electricity flowing through me. It was awesome to feel. The truth of what I spoke still rests inside of me. **That great evil will not overcome the earth, but Christ will overcome this evil.**

Jesus said in *Matthew 13:31-32*, **"The Kingdom of Heaven is like a mustard seed, which a man took and planted in his field. Though it is the smallest of all seeds, yet when it grows, it is the largest of garden plants and becomes a tree, so that the birds come and perch in its branches."**

Consider for a moment the words you just read. Please think about what Jesus was declaring. He said the Kingdom tree is the biggest tree in the garden. When I read this recently a light came on and I stopped worrying about the takeover of the planet by Islam. In fact, I am not worried about that at all now.

Christianity is the largest faith worldwide and will continue to be because Jesus declared it so while He was on the earth. Are you reading this? Don't worry about this present darkness because God is about to revive the earth so that even the persecutors are about to turn to him in mass.

Will you be a part of this revival? Will you go into the earth in this hour? Will you accept the call of Christ? Jesus is calling so who are the warriors that will rise?

CHAPTER 6

THIS IS THE HOUR OF THE COMING WATERS! HOW YOU CAN BECOME A CONDUIT OF IT IN YOUR LIFETIME

In a recent dream, I was standing on the edge of a great lake in Canada. I was astonished to see that the waters had receded so far that the shoreline had moved by hundreds of feet. I heard somebody in the dream say, "The waters have gone down by 150 feet," and they said this with a lot of fear as if the waters were gone forever.

As I was standing there, I was aware that this fear was in many hearts, so I said to the people near me, "Don't worry, these waters will be replenished. They shall come again."

I felt that the number 150 was significant and was somehow pointing to Scripture, so I went to the Bible and read Psalm 150. The passage was quite interesting, and I believe it is a key to the coming rise of the waters of the Spirit.

Psalm 150

Praise the Lord.
Praise God in His sanctuary;
praise Him in His mighty heavens.
Praise Him for His acts of power;
praise Him for His surpassing greatness.
Praise Him with the sounding of the trumpet,
praise Him with the harp and lyre,
praise Him with timbrel and dancing,
praise Him with the strings and pipe,
praise Him with the clash of cymbals,
praise Him with resounding cymbals.
Let everything that has breath praise the Lord.
Praise the Lord.

How to Replenish the Waters in Your Life

If we want the waters to be replenished our focus must be always and only on God. We must not look at the drought that is in the land or the people that are not worshipping Him. We must continue to focus on the God that took out Goliath and the God who split the Red Sea. He is the God that opened up the tomb and raised Jesus from the dead. He is the God that showed up in the upper room and filled the 120 with His holy presence so that they would become witnesses to the ends of the earth.

Our life must be a life filled with praise so that even when dark times are in our land, and even when it seems that the darkness is growing darker, our focus is on God and not the darkness at all. We need to fear and worship God above all things. Our hearts must move toward Him: to the God within the Holy Sanctuary, to the God of the mighty heavens above, to the God who acts with great power and who fears no one. When our meditation turns toward Him, then the problems of this world will fade away.

I was watching a film recently about Josephine Bakhita who was made a saint because of her devotion to Christ and love for people. She was born in the Sudan in 1869 and was captured as a slave. Her masters often beat her. At one point in her life, she rarely went without an open wound on her body because of the cruelty of her masters. By the grace of God she made it to Italy, and in 1890 entered a convent where she spent the rest of her life serving the Lord.

She was once asked by a student what she would say to her captors if she had the chance. She replied, "If I were to meet those who kidnapped me, and even those who tortured me, I would kneel and kiss their hands. For, if these things had not happened, I would not have been a Christian and a religious today."

This kind of praise and this kind of heart will never be enslaved in this present darkness. This is the heart of those who have truly overcome in Christ.

You Can Become a Conduit of the Waters in Your Lifetime

We must praise Him, and then we must continue to praise Him, and then we must praise Him some more. You will face many sufferings in this present life, but when you do, then do as the Apostle James said and *"***Consider it pure joy...** **whenever you face trials of many kinds***"* (*James 1:2*) because this will help you to overcome each trial.

As you practice praise at all times, and not just when it is convenient, the waters will return and many will be touched by God through your life as they were touched by God through Bakhita's life. **Even though she was a slave and had every right in the natural to be bitter and hate, she chose the way of love. She became a joy to many people, helping them to reach the place of intimacy with Christ in their own lives. She helped replenish the waters in her own time. We need to be that conduit in ours.**

John 7:38 says, *"***Whoever believes in Me, as Scripture has said, rivers of living water will flow from within them**.*"* These rivers are accessed through praise.

If I have learned anything about these waters in my own life, it is that as I look to my God my situation always changes. No matter what I face and no matter how difficult it seems, when my face turns to my God I am set free.

I remember many times when it felt like I could not make another single step because of the hopelessness in my heart, but when I turned my eyes upon Jesus and looked full into His wonderful face, my own slavery ended. Peace would come sweeping over me and tears would rush down my face as Jesus entered more deeply into my reality.

I have been blessed to have had a ministry that now has touched thousands of lives. It is not me that these people are longing to see, but God. As I point Heavenward toward Him, then He manifests Himself to the people, and the same God who healed and delivered me delivers and heals them.

As Psalm 150 shows, the key is always praise; and what seems fitting to me is that this is the last Psalm and it points Heavenward, to the eternal sanctuary, to the God of wonders, and to the God of all power. The waters will be replenished as we worship Him in all things.

And it seems certain to me that this is the hour of the coming waters when the great disparity in the earth will be repaired when the tides of this present darkness will be turned back as the Church rises into its destiny, spreading the love of Christ abroad to many hearts.

CHAPTER 7

DREAMS OF THE HARVEST: A MIGHTY HARVEST OF SOULS IS ABOUT TO TAKE PLACE!

Dreams of Salvations

I have had a number of dreams and visions in the last while which suggests to me that we are about to enter into a great "harvest of souls". About three weeks ago I had a dream while I was actually in Texas, near Austin. I was standing at the edge of a great river in the mountains. The waters were rushing dark and cold and, all of a sudden, I saw fish beginning to teem out of the waters of the river. It was a wondrous thing to behold. I started to cry in amazement because I could feel the Holy Spirit upon the waters.

Ezekiel 47:9 says, *"**Swarms of living creatures will live wherever the river flows. There will be large numbers of fish because this water flows there and makes the salt water fresh; so where the river flows everything will live***."*

Wherever the presence of God goes, the resurrection power of Jesus Christ begins to enter into dead lives. Waters that were putrid and salty become sweet in the Spirit of God. Those that were marked for the grave and Hell begin to bloom into spirits filled with the presence of God who will live for eternity with Christ their King.

Only a few times in my life have I seen waters teeming with fish. I remember once when I was in university studying my master's degree, I went to the ocean to help my friend paint his sailboat. While in the marina painting, a school of mackerel began to swim past our location. There were literally thousands of fish flapping and bubbling out of the water. It was so amazing to watch. I had no idea what I was witnessing, and had to be told, but the memory of that moment lives on within me.

When I was a boy in Labrador, Canada, I went on a fishing expedition into the wilderness with my Cub Scout's unit. There were about 30 or 40 of us boys with our leaders. We went fishing on a lake where only a few people ever seemed to go. Standing at the water's edge, I could literally see hundreds of fish in the water. It was so exciting to see so much life. These are the things you never forget.

The coming revival of Jesus Christ will be much more exciting. Jesus said, **"Follow Me, and I will make you fishers of men**" (*Matthew 4:19*).

I also had a dream recently in which I started to find gemstones all over the floor. Everywhere I looked there were different colored stones. I kept finding more and more. I felt that this was a prophetic image of the coming gathering of souls. *First Peter 2:5* says, *"***You also, like living stones, are being built into a spiritual house to be a holy priesthood,** offering spiritual sacrifices acceptable to God through Jesus Christ."

I believe that these stones that I was finding in my dream were salvations that are about to take place.

God Qualified You Through the Blood of Jesus to be Fishers and Harvesters

Jesus said, *"The harvest is plentiful, but the workers are few. Ask the Lord of the harvest, therefore, to send out workers into His harvest field"* (*Luke 10:2*).

I count myself as one who is sold out for the harvest, but the laborers are indeed few. **God wants to raise up people who will say** *yes* **to the harvest. You don't have to worry about being qualified because God qualifies you through the Blood of Jesus.**

Long before man recognized my ministry, I was leading people to Christ. My prayer is that many thousands of wild warriors of Christ will be released in this hour to help bring in the harvest. I am convinced that it will and that I shall see the ingathering of millions of souls into the harvest.

I remember many years ago standing on a porch looking at a farmer's field. No one in those days would have me to preach, but I used to imagine that field filled with thousands of souls, and they were coming to Christ.

And since that time I have preached to thousands world-wide. **God was faithful to the vision of the harvest that**

He gave to me. The word of God in my heart says that I will see much more than this. I can see millions of souls in my heart, and I know that I will see many of them touched by the power of God.

I went to see the new movie by Affirm Films called "Risen" with my sons a couple of days ago, starring Joseph Fiennes. This is the story of the resurrection of Jesus Christ as told through the eyes of a Roman Tribune who was investigating the missing corpse. In the end, he was convinced, of course, that Christ rose from the dead – but there is this great scene in the movie where the disciples are waiting for Christ in Galilee and they get hungry, so they get into the boats and move out upon the waters to catch a harvest of fish.

You know the story as well as I do. They fished all night and found nothing. In the morning Christ was standing on the shore and told them to throw the net out onto the other side of the boat. And, of course, so many fish enter into the net the boat almost capsized under the weight of them.

This is what we are about to see. We are about to see a mighty harvest of souls that will fill every church to brimming. In fact, the churches will not be able to hold the souls that are coming. Houses will be filled with them. I have seen and heard that stadiums will be filled. The Lord is releasing an anointing in this hour for stadiums. Many millions will come to the Lord this way.

What I loved about the movie *Risen* and, indeed, any movie that depicts the disciples of Christ, is how their faces do not stand out any more than any other face. What is wonderful is that we do not know what they looked like. They could have looked like you and me. In fact, they were just like us. **They had an encounter with Christ that changed them and they were filled with the Holy Spirit that empowered them to do the extraordinary in their times.**

I pray that God will fill us the same way in this hour and a great boldness will come upon us to see the harvest brought in.

WOMEN ARE RISING IN MINISTRY!

In a number of dreams over the last month, I have seen how God wants to use women to bring in the end-time harvest of the Lord.

"Don't Stop Revival"

In the first dream I saw how God wanted to start a revival in a major city in America, but it was stopped because the leaders of that city could not recognize the package that God wanted to use. In this dream, I saw the Holy Spirit begin to rise on a young woman. She was given the mic to begin to speak and prophesy, but as she started to manifest under the power of the Holy Spirit, the leaders were not comfortable because they thought she was of the flesh, so they took the mic away from her. She literally ran toward me crying and saying, "You don't understand; they just stopped revival from coming to this great city." I consoled her and said, "I do understand, this has also happened to me in the past."

I want you to consider this dream for a moment. I wonder how many revivals in the earth have been stopped before they could even happen. How many souls have been lost as a result?

When I was young, I heard a story in Halifax, Nova Scotia. There was a revival preacher in the early 1900's that was seeing great results as he preached around Atlantic Canada. As he neared Nova Scotia, the leaders of the church put a stop to him coming in. They were not happy with the message he was preaching and the way he was preaching it. As a result, the revival he was a part of didn't come into that land.

The truth is we don't always like the packages that God wants to use to bring in revival. I know of churches in my own region that would never consider that revival could move anywhere other than inside their doors, but inside their churches, the Holy Spirit is not allowed to move. I won't pretend to understand why they stop God from moving. Perhaps they have been hurt in the past. Perhaps they have seen it all before.

And some of the wildest packages that God will use in this hour for revival will be women.

General William Booth, the founder of the Salvation Army, is known to have said, "Some of my best men are women!" I remember when I was young hearing his granddaughter speak in Newfoundland, Canada. The church was filled with people wanting to hear this woman's stories of her grandfather. It was thrilling to hear her. There was a soaring in the spirit that day.

Pray and Intercede – Your Authority with the King!

In another recent dream, I saw 1 Kings 2:19: "Bathsheba, therefore, went to King Solomon, to speak to him for Adonijah. And the king rose up to meet her and bowed down to her, and sat down on his throne and had a throne set for the king's mother; so she sat at his right hand."

I want you to consider the picture that is being painted in this passage. Bathsheba approaches her son, the king, to intercede on behalf of another son. When she comes into the throne room where her son is seated, he greets her by standing. He then has a throne brought to her so that she can sit in the presence of the king. This is a picture of the authority this woman had with her son.

I feel that this is a picture of what God wants to do with women in this hour. I believe that women are about to be granted an authority to sit in the presence of the King to intercede on behalf of others. Women who will sit in the presence of the King, seeking His voice and pleasure, will become like the salt that was thrown into the waters of Jericho. In 2 Kings 2:19-22, Elisha was in Jericho where he was staying after Elijah was brought up to Heaven in a chariot. One of the first miracles that he performed was throwing salt from a new bowl into the waters of Jericho which purified them for generations.

For me, the bowl represents the vessels that God uses to pray and intercede, and what is inside of them is the power of the Holy Spirit to change things.

This passage in 2 Kings reminds me of the image that is painted in the book of Revelation 5:8 which says, "...the four living creatures and the twenty-four elders fell down before the Lamb. Each one had a harp and they were holding golden bowls full of incense, which are the prayers of God's people."

This is a picture of the power of intercession that I believe is rising in the hearts of women in this hour. God is going to use them to purify the impure waters of towns. Their prayers are going to be so powerful that towns, cities and indeed entire regions will be shifted into purity for generations. God has ordained a season for the Church. This is the hour of the Army of God rising. He is going to use ordinary people to do extraordinary things for His glory because He can.

This is a picture of warfare in the spirit. I declare that women will even have mighty dreams and visions of the conflict that is taking place. They will see by the Holy Spirit the battle and they will be a part of it, inflicting great devastation and harm on the plans of the enemy in this hour. We must always remember that our battle is not against flesh and blood, but against the powers, rulers and authorities in the heavenly realms (*Ephesians 6:12).*

Your prayers have the power to shift atmospheres and bring in the glory of God. I declare that the women of God shall be an instrument yielded and wielded in the hands of the King to produce a new sound that will change nations.

Miracles, Healings, and Deliverances!

All this shall be bathed in the love of Jesus. The nurturing hearts of women shall perform miracles, healing, and deliverance, as they are filled with the love of Christ. They shall prophesy and they shall walk in the gifts of the Spirit. They will become the mothers, daughters, and sisters that the earth has been groaning for since the beginning of creation.

A prayer for women today: I pray that God would open you up to new levels of glory. I ask the Lord to move you into a greater understanding of His love and His grace. I pray that the revelation of the King will fill your heart so that your prayers will be powerful and effective, and may the blessing of our God overlap and fill you completely.

CHAPTER 8

PROPHECY OF THE KNIGHTS IN WHITE LINEN: YOU ARE THE KNIGHTS!

As of recently, the Lord keeps bringing a phrase into my heart. He has been telling me that **the people of God are about to rise as warriors of the Cross and they shall be known as "Knights in White Linen."**

On a recent morning as I was washing the dishes, that phrase kept rolling in my heart in the form of a song. I must have sung it hundreds of times before it entered into my mind as a thought. I believe angels were singing it to me. They are excited about the prospect of the coming of these mighty ones.

I began to do some research on this phrase and came to a nice little verse in Revelation 19:14. In this passage, a wonderful picture is painted of the armies of Heaven following Christ into battle. It says, "The armies of Heaven were following Him, riding on white horses and dressed in fine linen, white and clean."

These armies have been washed in the Blood of the lamb. These are the souls of the departed saints that are going to return with Christ when He invades this world and destroys the armies of darkness.

The Lord in this hour is about to send His fire upon the Church. Those that are not ready may not be prepared for this fire, but it is going to consume the darkness from their lives. They are going to be touched in the core of their beings and they will rise as Knights in White Linen. They will conquer darkness in the name of the King.

You Are a Conqueror!

You are royalty in Christ. You are undefeatable in Christ. There is nothing that can conquer you. You are more than a conqueror. You are an overcomer who will overcome every trial and difficulty that is in your life.

I often hear people talk about the trials that they are going through like they cannot overcome them. You need to know that you are not alone. Everyone goes through difficulty. Everyone has something that they are facing which they must endure and overcome. Maybe it is a health situation or a crisis in the family. Maybe it is a financial situation, or your neighbor or boss is treating you harshly. Whatever the problem, you have Christ as the answer.

As we allow Him to wash us clean of all the stains in our hearts then we will be prepared for the new thing that God has for our lives. It is not that we do anything to make ourselves worthy. Jesus did it all on the Cross.

Your job is to stand and respond to the prompting of the Holy Spirit. He will speak to your heart and say things like, "Perhaps it is time to stop hating your neighbor." You will say, "Yes Lord, You are right, please forgive me." As we respond to the issues He places before us, He will set us free of many things that have been holding us down.

Just let God touch the deep places of your heart. You can feel the pain in there. Place yourself in a position to let him lift every burden from your life. Lie face down in the glory and tell Him you want to be changed. He will change you day by day. Just let go and let Him wash away the pain of your life.

1 John 1:7 says, "But if we walk in the light, as He is in the light, we have fellowship with one another, and the Blood of Jesus, His Son, cleanses us from all sin."

And then there is this gem of a verse in Hebrews 9:14, "How much more will the Blood of Christ, who through the eternal Spirit offered Himself without blemish to God, purify our conscience from dead works to serve the living God."

And again in Ephesians 5:26-27, "...that He might sanctify her, having cleansed her by the washing of water with the Word, so that He might present the Church to Himself in splendor, without spot or wrinkle or any such thing, that she might be holy and without blemish."

You are a part of this army of God that is rising. Jesus is going to cleanse every spot and wrinkle of your life. You are a Knight in White Linen. The work of Jesus on the Cross is sufficient to cleanse and set you free.

A prayer over you: *I declare that every blockage that has kept you down will now be unblocked and you will be victorious in the next season. The sin that trapped you and kept you in shame and guilt will be destroyed because of what Jesus did on the Cross. Get ready for your deliverance. Get ready for new freedom.*

CHAPTER 9

A PILGRIM'S VOYAGE HAS A WAY OF INCREASING YOUR FAITH AND TRUST IN GOD

<u>Set on Pilgrimage</u>

The pursuit of the Lord is the greatest thing. Early in my Christian walk, I read *Psalm 84:5* which says, **"Blessed is the man whose strength is in You, whose heart is set on pilgrimage."** When I read this, the idea of Pilgrimage began to echo in my heart. Inside of me began an earnest desire to travel the earth finding places where I could encounter the Lord Most High.

You can connect with Christ anywhere and certainly will, but for me, my life has become a journey and I go from place to place seeking God through the people that He brings my way. I have found that the expression of Christ is different from culture to culture, and as I journey through the Body of Christ, my expression of Christ becomes more rich and full.

In the last 11 months, I have been in 14 nations. Each country is now a part of my experience. I have friends in all of these places. I love the way the Holy Spirit moves through them. We have laughed together and we have cried together. These people have become a part of my family and I love them dearly.

I have learned through the years that God has been with me as I have set my feet toward pilgrimage. In fact, I believe now that many of the steps I took were not my own but straight from the heart of God. The knowledge that I have stepped into has changed me for the better. My heart is now more open to the world.

There are places in the world that still frighten me, but as I journey to each new place my old fears have a way of fading away. Many people are afraid of traveling, especially in this day in Europe where there have been many terrorist attacks, but I have now been to places in Europe that feel safer than Canada. If I had not traveled here I would not have learned that and that fear of terror would have continued to grip me.

The Lord has been putting in my heart the countries of the old Silk Road. These are the countries that extend between China in the East and Turkey in the West. There are many countries on the old Silk Road. There is 12,000 km of land where hundreds of millions of people live. These are very Muslim lands. If I am to travel there with the Gospel, I am going to have to face new fears; but if God places these things in our hearts, will He not keep us safe when we go there? The answer to this question is answered by going. You will only know if God will keep you safe by *going*.

Pilgrimage has a way of increasing your faith and trust in God.

Recently I was eating a meal when a bone splinter got caught in my throat here in Greece. It was the shape of a toothpick and it got just above my breathing passage. In a moment like that, you can panic very easily, but I heard the Lord say, "Remain calm." Panic would have made the situation worse and I might have completely swallowed the bone. As I remained calm, I was able to cough the bone out very easily. I understood from this experience that God was able to protect me even in faraway lands.

On the island of Crete, I walked into a church that was deep inside of a cave in St. Nikolaos. This town is very pretty, and at the heart of it, there is a saltwater lake with many small fishing vessels ready to go to sea. The Greek Orthodox Church has many small chapels and churches in Greece. These are places where pilgrims can go inside and pray. I have prayed in many such places.

Inside of this church, I needed my flashlight because it was very dark. I had some fear and vain imaginings as I stepped into the furthest part of the cave. It got darker and darker. My mind began to see demons everywhere I looked. I wanted to turn around and go back, but I didn't want fear to stop me, so I kept walking deeper into the cave.

At the end of the cave, there was another little cave and I stepped into it. There, lying on the ground and surrounded by the darkest dark, were five or six Eastern Orthodox paintings done in gold paint. I was thinking these could be stolen so easily. There was one of Jesus surrounded by the Holy Spirit while others depicted scenes from the Bible like Peter jumping out onto the water. These were, in fact, great treasures. I was glad that I didn't turn when afraid or I would not have seen these amazing treasures.

Fear has a way of stopping us from entering places where great surprises are waiting for us.

I told my friends that I thought it was strange how the paintings were just lying there. He told me that the Cretans would never steal these paintings because they believe if they do bad luck would come upon them as a curse.

I learned on my journey that the island of Crete has the oldest European settlement and that civilization spread from there. There is a ruin in Knossos that is almost 4,000 years old. These were descendants of Noah.

In Irakleion, Crete, which in English translates into *Hercules*, there are many mountains. While there, I saw one mountain covered in snow. One of my friends told me that this was where Zeus was born and then he pointed to another mountain and told me that is where Zeus went to school. There was yet a third mountain in that town and it looks like a man's face. They call it the Face of Zeus, and human sacrifices were performed behind that mountain to appease the gods. Twice this beautiful city was destroyed by earthquakes, and my friend said that he felt it was judgment for the idolatry that occurred there.

It was strange being in that town where the religion of Zeus began. I told the people that I was excited being there because in our day Zeus seems to be gaining power and notoriety again in North America with depictions of him in many modern films. **I told the people I was happy to be in the place of his birth so that I could remind them that Jesus Christ was still Lord.**

Seeing all these things has a way of changing you. You become stronger, and the only way to see these things is by becoming a pilgrim. **A pilgrim has no choice but to trust the Lord.**

I pray that you will also enter into the journey and that God will open up your steps to the world.

CHAPTER 10

A NEW SHIFT IN OUR THOUGHTS THAT WILL LIBERATE MANY!

<u>A Vision of Entering into a New Place</u>

Recently I was in England ministering at a Methodist Church in Sheffield. The leader of that group had the people soak for an hour to anointed worship before the speaker got up to share. It had been a while since I had laid down on the floor and waited upon the Lord. At first, I didn't think I would bother but then I thought why not? I found a nice little spot where I could just lie down and wait upon the Lord. (I remember years ago spending many hours soaking to the Holy Spirit and to anointed music.)

Well, I was down on the floor for no longer than a few minutes when suddenly, I went into a wonderful trance. I saw myself walking down a road and then I made a turn and what I saw was absolutely amazing. It was evening time and I was making a turn onto a street I had never been down before. The sun was setting and the light was filling up the entire street. The sun radiated off of the buildings up and down that road.

It was the glory of God. I could sense this incredible Spirit of the Lord as I made the turn. A new hope rose up in me as I began to walk down that road. In fact, I know that in the vision, I had been walking for quite some time before I got to this turn but when I did it was as if my life and energy were renewed. I joyfully stepped into that new road and felt refreshing come strongly into my heart.

I do sense that we are entering into a new season starting in this very moment. I believe that many in the Body are about to enter into some new thoughts that are going to liberate them to walk in greater places for the Lord.

Pay Attention to New Thoughts Coming Your Way

What I have come to realize recently is that anytime something new begins in our life it begins as a new thought. Our thoughts are the place where God speaks so that liberty will flow into our lives and then we will step into the things that He has in store for us.

Nothing that I have done for Christ was by accident.

Every step that I have taken has started in my mind. Jesus provides direction to those who diligently seek and follow Him. When you begin to seek Christ, His thoughts begin to flow through your mind. It is one thing to have the thought but it is another to enter into it.

Many of the best ideas and thoughts that I have ever written or spoken began as a whisper in my ear. I have often awakened with a pen in my hand to jot down the words that have entered into my heart through the night hours, like a voice in my ear.

He makes us look good as we speak and as we obey His voice. There is a brilliance and a wisdom that only comes from the heart of God. His light within us is His wisdom and this understanding. In fact, all wisdom and understanding come from God. These are a part of the Seven Spirits of God. When we embrace that wisdom, our path is illuminated and we begin to enter into the greater promises for our life.

I was in Berlin, Germany recently and had a wonderful encounter with the Lord at a street front church. As I was prophesying over the people I went into a vision and saw the candles of Heaven descend upon the people of Berlin. There was such wonder in this encounter.

A Word for Germany

The Lord began to speak to me and say that: **Germany was about to enter its greatest hour for Christ**. I saw that new ideas were about to enter into the minds of the next generation of philosophers and theologians that will break the power of darkness that came in the last century.

This will be a reformation in thought. These people will be filled with the seven spirits of God and they will be like lighthouses that shine their light so that all that enter into it will be rescued and saved.

There will be an unfolding of a new but ancient wisdom from God. It will be new in the sense that those that are of this generation will begin to hear God's truth spoken to them in a way that they can understand.

I felt that Germany was to be a place where the candles burned brightly and where the angelic realm operated in a way that brought great deliverance to the minds of men. I saw that those that will operate in Germany underneath this reformation spirit will become wise and remembered as reformers in their time.

A New Turn Bringing Deliverance to Minds

This is the new turn that I believe we are all about to enter into. I feel strongly that there is coming a wave of the Presence to drive out all that is wrong in intellectualism in this hour. The philosophies that have entered into a generation and brought them far from the Cross of Christ will be exposed as the heresies they are. Jesus will shine brightly and His wisdom will appear brilliant and simple at the same time.

I cannot emphasize enough the well-being I felt as I saw these candles being revealed to the hearts of men. I could see the very chains begin to fall as they entered into these new and brilliant thoughts. This path that is opening in this hour is going to be amazing.

The light of God revealed to the hearts of men bringing freedom to all who embrace it.

2 Corinthians 4:6: For God, who said, "**Let light shine out of darkness**," made His light shine in our hearts to give us the light of the knowledge of God's glory displayed in the face of Christ.

I believe that before we enter into the great reformation there has to be a shift in the thoughts of mankind. What God revealed in the past revivals was excellent and heavenly, but He wants to reveal more in this hour.

Who are the ones that will put themselves to the task to wait and listen to His voice? I sense the young men and women of this generation are about to rise.

I was in Howarth, England where a great revival took place under a couple of amazing reformers named John and Charles Wesley. I was told that as John spoke to a church in that town, 2000 people were present inside of the church, and then there were 6000 more standing outside, some of them on scaffolding to hear what this amazing preacher had to say. I asked a friend why this revival took place and they said, "John Wesley was not afraid to preach the Gospel even if it offended."

That is the heart of the reformer. There is fearlessness within them. I pray that you will become like this and that God's fire will begin to burn in you for the entire world to see.

CHAPTER 11

REVIVAL IN CANADA! GOD IS RAISING UP THE GOOD SHEPHERDS WHO WILL BRING IN THE SHEEP

This word is boiling to the service this morning! I am very excited in the spirit of what God is about to do. This morning many of the prophetic images that I have had over the last while are colliding together and I am seeing a clearer picture. About two months ago or more, I had a dream in which I was seeing "revival meetings break out in Canada". I was not in the country when this was happening but as soon as I got back I joined in the meetings. One of my friends was there and when I went into the meeting I stood beside him.

The name of the speaker in these meetings was "Victoria". She was dynamic and filled with the Holy Spirit. I remember seeing the glory lights fill the meeting space which happened to be taking place in a tent. A tent to me speaks of something temporary.

On May 29-31, 2015, I was with Doug Addison, Steve Shultz, and Patricia Bootsma at the Canadian Elijah List Conference in Hamilton, Ontario, Canada. This was Joe and Bella Garcia's Church, "The River International Church." Doug began to prophesy that something big was going to take place in the Hamilton and the Greater Toronto region on May 20, 2016. In Canada, the May 20th weekend is known as the Victoria Day long weekend. It is the celebration of Queen Victoria of England. So could this be the Victoria from my dream? I think that is the interpretation.

There are meetings starting this weekend May 27 to June 1 in Hamilton at the same church where Doug prophesied. These were not planned a year ago. Todd Bentley has been seeing a major revival in Edmonton and decided he wanted to cross Canada and Joe and Bella Garcia's Church, The River International, is where he is going. This was decided in the last week or so.

This morning as I was waking I saw a vision. In it, there was a shepherd – a very healthy and spry looking shepherd who had a great stride and bounce in his step. He was carrying a walking step which he was using to guide the sheep. This was the sort of fellow I would have expected to see herding sheep in the high hills of Northern England and Scotland. In the vision, the sheep were walking beside him and they were running to keep up. He was determinedly guiding them to shelter.

Then there is another image that came to me also this morning. I saw a video on Facebook of eagles gathering together fishing. Each, in turn, would leap from the air toward the ocean waters to gather a fish within its beak.

God is saying that "something is about to happen in the spirit." He is about to raise up the good shepherds who will bring in the sheep and catch the fish. There is an acceleration occurring in this moment for the harvest. I believe that we are going to see an increase in activity in the next while. We will also see the gathering of the prophets for harvest. Many will start coming together and in that place of association, there will come an open Heaven for what God is doing.

I believe that with the Victoria Day weekend in Canada, we actually crossed a window into a different place spiritually. **We have entered into the harvest zone, so get ready to hear reports of increased activities for harvest. There will be more fires about to burn in new places.**

I must stress that I really feel the Lord is saying that "we must join together to see this harvest of souls." We must act as one Body. We must gather and we must engage the enemy as one force. The enemy has taken out people in the past when they operate as lone rangers. I am seeing a picture of harvest in community with each other.

This is not only for the harvest but for your well-being. One of the great marks of revival is supernatural fellowship. I have seen this everywhere I go. People will even move from towns into new towns in order to be in the place where the Spirit of God is moving in community. I saw that occur in the revival that I was a part of in Kinburn, Ontario under Mark Redner. People will move to hot spots in order to serve and to have divine fellowship. I believe that we will see this again in this season.

Todd Bentley has been seeing "the Glory Train" a lot lately. The Glory Train is an image that stays with me. It never leaves. I have been seeing it for 12 years ever since I came back to Christ. I once saw the Glory Train in a vision steaming up the valley where I live in. I knew it was a sign of revival and indeed that is what we experienced in those years.

Yesterday as I was praying into what God is doing in Hamilton, I came to the decision in prayer that I was completely behind what God is going to do there, even though physically I am going to be in Australia for the next two months carrying out revival services there. However, I decided that whatever I could do in social media to advance what God is doing there then I will do it.

As I ended my prayer, as I was praying in my art studio, I came into the house and began to write an endorsement for the meetings. I attached the poster that was developed for the meetings to what I had written which was a pic of a Glory Train and then I sent it out. I went into the kitchen where my kids had been painting all morning and my six-year-old son who is very prophetic came up to me with a picture he had done. First I was not paying attention to him but he was relentless and insisted that I look. Finally, he said, "Dad, look I have painted the Glory Train."

I was shocked. I had no idea that he was painting it, and what is more, he even knew to call it the Glory Train. God is speaking if we will listen. God is about to move in power in Canada once again. It is time for something fresh in the spirit. It is time for the convocation of the eagles for harvest. Get ready for great gatherings to take place and for many to be brought into the Kingdom as a result.

I pray that the enemy will not distract this move of the Holy Spirit and I pray that you will have eyes to see and a heart to embrace what God is doing. You may not be one hundred percent comfortable with the packages that God wants to use but I pray that will not stop you from stepping in. Some of you need to hear this as you step into what God is about to do: your entire family is going to be saved. So I pray that you will be strengthened and softened to enter into what the Spirit is doing.

CHAPTER 12

THE RISING OF THE AGING WARRIORS

I just had a vision of the older generation. I see that many who are in their 50's and higher have been battling the thoughts of the enemy for a long time. Many of you have been gripped with chains of depression, anxiety, and fear. Some of you may have resorted to substance abuse and even medication in order to cope with the weight that came against you.

However, the battle in the mind is actually a battle in the spirit. You have been in the middle of an incredible battle and you have barely held your ground but you will hold your ground. You will be like David's mighty man Shammah.

2 Samuel 23:11-12 says, **"One time the Philistines gathered at Lehi and attacked the Israelites in a field full of lentils. The Israelite army fled, but Shammah held his ground in the middle of the field and beat back the Philistines. So the Lord brought about a great victory."**

There is a mighty valor that rises in the hearts of God's people when they determine to stand their ground despite the coming onslaught before them. You may be going through a difficult time on the job. You may be facing persecution from family for your faith. You may not have enough money to get to the end of the week and the landlord is threatening to throw you out, but if you stand your ground in faith none of these things will overcome you. You will triumph every time in Christ.

Bursting into the Realm of God's Light

Just recently I saw a vision of a man's head bursting through the iron clouds of darkness into the eternal realm of God's light and love. I actually saw this amazing amber light glow as his head went into the realm of God's presence.

You see, the victory for your breakthrough has already been established. When Jesus died on the Cross, your salvation was secure in Him, but the battle lies in the thoughts. If the enemy can keep your mind on earthly things and bound to his lies then you will not overcome. But if you seek God He will fill you with His glorious thoughts and you will rule and reign in Him.

I watched as this man's head burst into the stratosphere of God's blinding light and all darkness began to fall off of him. You need to continue to seek God until you find Him. There is no point in giving up. You have to stand up and fight another day.

Each morning when you wake, ask God for His thought for the day. He will guide you and you will overcome. He has good treasures in store for your life... so many of them that you would never be able to imagine them let alone count them.

I know that many in the older generation have been pressing into the things of God for a long time, but they have learned to persevere as a result.

I declare that if you are one of these then you will become some of the greatest dragon slayers of our time. The dragons are the thoughts that would destroy the minds of mankind. Once you have broken into the realm of God's presence and glory you will help others do the same. You will become the greatest peacemakers and encouragers. You will become the lifters of broken hearts and minds.

When we get the victory in Jesus, this victory becomes the potential victory for many others. I pray that you will continue to persevere so that you will become hardened to the enemies tactics and alive in the things of God. I pray that His great hope will awaken your senses so that you begin to fight like never before.

The truth is: Your greatest days are before you.

CHAPTER 13

THE WONDERS OF ALMIGHTY GOD

Our God is amazing. There is no one who performs the mighty wonders that He performs. There is no one who can split the waters, turn the water into wine, or heal the sick like our God. I was in Montreal recently where I encountered some incredible miracles of the Lord.

Acts 2:19 says, **"I will show wonders in the heavens above and signs in the earth beneath."**

Four days before I went to Montreal, hundreds of people heard on the west side of the city what sounded like trumpets blasting in the sky. In fact, the dogs were particularly upset.

There is actually a recording of this phenomenon that was posted to the city's main Online Newspaper, the Montreal Gazette. **I heard it and was enlivened by it. It really sounded like trumpets. I believe that the Lord is announcing a new day in the earth and the return of the dominance of the King. Revival is taking place and millions of souls are coming to Christ all through Quebec and around the world.**

An Atmosphere of Miracles

The meetings that we had in Montreal were beyond wild. There were miracles in those meetings I have never seen before. I was one of two invited speakers at a conference emphasizing the Holy Spirit called "Dunamis." There were close to 1000 people present and most of them saw one of the miracles that was taking place. Theresa de Jesus L. is a powerful woman of God originally from Guatemala but is now living in California and she walks in oil miracles.

She has a Bible that was literally soaked with scented oils from Heaven. I am told that she sometimes gives her Bible away and when she gets a new one the same thing happens again. She actually spent three days in prison in North Korea because of this but was released when the guards saw a spiritual being in her cell. They got scared and thought she was a witch so they let her go.

I actually got to touch some of this oil. It was an amazing miracle to behold. When you are in an atmosphere of miracles nothing seems impossible. I love being around people like Theresa who just believe God is who He says He is and can do whatever He wants.

These miracles show the power of the Gospel. Jesus came to die for you and me so that we could live a transformed life. Did you know that the same Spirit that raised Jesus from the dead lives in you and in me (*Romans 8:11*)? This is the Holy Spirit and He is working in your life to resurrect every dead part of it.

When you turn to Christ, you turn to a God that is able to free you from depression, fear, and anxiety. You turn to a God that is able to heal your body and your mind. In Christ, you will be baptized in the peace and joy of God. Your every morning after will be filled with new hope for a new day.

Miracles follow the preaching of the message. This is the Good News of Christ. I have been prophesying that miracles were going to increase but when you begin to see this happen it still amazes you.

Are You Hungry For More of Him?

There was such an atmosphere of hunger in Montreal. People ran to the altars by the hundreds to get a touch from Christ and to see the miracles that were taking place. These people extended their hands toward me. They reminded me of the woman who wanted to touch the hem of Jesus' garment. They wanted an encounter with the glory of God for themselves.

When you see this kind of hunger it changes you. For me I have been in the glory so long it is normal now, but for these people, they were seeking God like it was their last day to touch the hem of His garment. It seemed like life and death for them.

I wonder about you dear reader...are you as hungry for the move of the Holy Spirit in your own life? There are people right now having amazing encounters all over the earth. My question for you is, "Are you going to seek God until you find Him?"

Recently in one of my meetings in Texas, a pearl was found on the floor that manifested out of Heaven. I was reminded in that moment that Jesus is the pearl of great price (*Matthew 13:45-46*). As you know the person in that parable sold all that they had in order to buy the field where this pearl was located. Are you as hungry? Are you willing to pay the price to encounter God?

Peter and John walked away from their nets (*Matthew 4:18-20*). They didn't care about the rewards of this earth. They saw Christ and felt the Presence all around them. They felt life for the first time by just being near to Him. They gladly forsook this life for the Kingdom.

But then there was the rich young ruler (*Matthew 19:16-22*). He came to Christ as a deacon of the church who could say in his heart that he had obeyed the precepts of Scripture and had kept the commandments. But when challenged to move into the greater sacrifice he couldn't do it. His heart was too bound to this world and to the luxuries of this life. He couldn't see beyond the blue sky. Even though he felt the mysteries of Heaven when in the presence of Christ, his fear of lack bound him. Instead of joining Christ and seeing marvelous moves of the Spirit for the rest of his life, he remained a deacon of a dead church.

God can warm your heart, but you have to seek him anew. You have to turn your eyes upon Jesus and look full into His wonderful face. I can assure you that the things of this world will grow strangely dim. His glory is worth the fight. What

He does in broken lives is the only thing that will last for eternity. Everything else will fade away.

I pray that you will have the courage and the boldness to step out in a new way in this hour. May God fill you with the assurance of His presence and may His fire come from Heaven and burn away every desire that is not from Him.

CHAPTER 14

THE MIGHTY HAMMER OF GOD FOR WAR

s I was ministering my first night in Australia, I saw something very interesting. It was as if a whirlwind came toward me and I could see within it many hammers that were coming to help the Church. These were the hammers of God.

Jeremiah 23:29 says, "**Is not My Word like fire,**" declares the Lord, "**and like a hammer that breaks a rock in pieces?**"

When I hear that the hammers are being released I believe that this is about destroying the lies and mindsets that hinder people from entering into the fullness of what God wants to do in their life. A hammer breaks down but also builds up.

When the voice of God comes He destroys darkness. When the sounds of Heaven enter into the earth realm the earth is transformed by the power of God. When the hammer of

God came to Ezekiel in the Valley of Dry Bones, the spirit of death was destroyed and the life of God came.

God destroyed death but built up life. When the hammer of God came to Paul on the road to Damascus, Paul's old nature was destroyed but new life began to rise in him in Christ. He became the greatest missionary of his generation.

When God's Hammer Comes...

When the hammers come, they break the rocks that try to hinder your great destiny. It can be a simple lie like, "You will never accomplish any good thing," but if you believe it, then it will stop you from entering into God's fullness. If you believe that you will always be poor then this can stop you from entering into the blessings that God has assigned to your life.

The hammers of God are an angelic host that comes from the throne of God to invade the earth realm. When Heaven speaks to earth, the earth is changed. The Kingdom of Heaven begins to manifest in this realm.

When the hammers come physical healing will come. When the hammers come people are delivered from evil. When the hammers come people begin to believe for the impossible. People go on great exploits. They have the strength to climb mountains, swim across great seas. There is nothing that can stop them.

When God's hammer comes and breaks the chains of doubt and oppression, the people of God rise up in the valor of the mighty men of old and begin to conquer in the name of Jesus Christ.

All victory begins with a Word from God. When the fire of the Word and the hammer manifests, darkness is destroyed in its wake. The enemy starts running because he knows the voice of God and he knows the people who know the voice of God. He will not mess with those that are filled with the Word.

And so I declare that over your life today that God is going to fill you up completely with His Word and you will become victorious in all your ways. You will also bring victory to many other people's lives in Jesus' mighty name. This is the goodness of the Lord in your life. You will not remain bound but victorious because of the work of the Cross.

So Father, send Your hammer to the people now.

CHAPTER 15

THE RAINBOW ANGEL AND NO MORE DELAY

<u>A Rainbow to Gibraltar</u>

O ver the last couple of months, I have been seeing a tremendous sign in the Heaven's above. On about four occasions in different locations around the world, I have seen wild rainbows. **I have come to think of it as a sign that God is saying that there is no more delay to revival.** (I will share why below.)

I was in Spain just over a month ago and drove from Malaga to Gibraltar. This is a very lovely drive near mountains and the sea which takes about one and half hours. As I left the airport, the gentlemen driving me, who was a missionary from Sweden, decided that he wanted to drive me along the sea.

We did so aboard a two-door convertible Peugeot. It was great fun. Not 10 minutes into the drive did a giant rainbow appear in the sky. There had been many storms in that area over the previous few days and the clouds were heavy on the

Eastern Horizon, but there was breakage in the clouds now, and it was getting close to sunset.

The rainbow was astounding. One side of the rainbow touched the earth and then arched all the way to the Mediterranean Sea. It amazed me. I had never seen the end of a rainbow touch the water in that matter before. I felt this was significant because I could feel the Holy Spirit in it, but didn't have any revelation as to what it could mean.

We had lovely meetings in Gibraltar. I was with a group of Charismatic Catholics linked to the Gibraltar House of Prayer. We prayed together and made declarations over Africa, Europe, the Atlantic Ocean and the Mediterranean Sea. **I declared that Jesus Christ was still on the throne and that the best days of revival were still ahead of us.**

Aboriginal Legend and Distorted Rainbow Meaning

Over 4 weeks ago, I arrived in Australia, where we have been having many revival meetings. We have been declaring that Christ shall reign in Australia all the way from the spiritual centre of Uluru (or Ayers Rock) to the seas on all sides.

We went to a place called Victor Harbor, which is about an hour drive from the city of Adelaide in South Australia. When we arrived, I saw the second great rainbow. It draped and touched the land on one side and touched the sea on the other side. The person that I was with thought nothing of it, but in my heart, I knew that it was not a coincidence that I was seeing the second such rainbow in a month.

Moreover, I have learned that the First Nations People of Australia considered the place where this rainbow appeared to be a sacred spot and named it after a god in their language (note: I share below how God is taking territory).

Granite Rock near Victor Harbor in the Aboriginal language is *Nulcoowarra* and was a place of great spiritual significance to the people. The Aboriginal religions had a common belief in the rainbow serpent which they call the creator. The serpent is linked to the worship of a fertility goddess. There are blood rituals linked to the worship of this being.

In one of the legends of this serpent, it falls to the earth like a meteor and creates a great crater. A hunter goes to the crater looking for the serpent in the tunnels it created and never comes out again. A Dingle accompanied him and was eaten and the bones were spat out of the cave.

Interesting also is how the homosexual community has used the rainbow flag. Some commentators cite a link between this rainbow serpent and the rainbow flag. It would seem that they are knowingly or unknowingly worshipping this goddess.

Rainbow - Biblical Promise and Blessing

You and I know though that the rainbow is a symbol from the Bible. When the rainbow appeared to Noah it was a promise that a flood would never destroy the earth again. In popular culture rainbows can be "signs of blessing and prosperity". I tend to think blessings when I see

rainbows and begin to declare them over the regions that I see them in.

While my family and I were driving in Australia, we saw a rainbow in the distance. I noticed that the end of the rainbow was over the road I was driving down. I said to my wife, "It looks like we are going to drive right through it." In fact, we did. As we got to the place where the rainbow was located, light came through the car. We felt that this was a sign of God's blessings to come.

I mentioned this rainbow to a lady in Adelaide, who is connected with the prayer network of Australia. She mentioned the Rainbow Angel to me from *Revelation 10:2-7:*

"Then I saw another mighty angel coming down from Heaven. He was robed in a cloud, with a rainbow above his head; his face was like the sun, and his legs were like fiery pillars. He was holding a little scroll, which lay open in his hand.

He planted his right foot on the sea and his left foot on the land, and he gave a loud shout like the roar of a lion. When he shouted, the voices of the seven thunders spoke. And when the seven thunders spoke, I was about to write; but I heard a voice from Heaven say, 'Seal up what the seven thunders have said and do not write it down.'

"Then the angel I had seen standing on the sea and on the land raised his right hand to Heaven. And he swore by Him who lives forever and ever, who created the heav-

ens and all that is in them, the earth and all that is in it, and the sea and all that is in it, and said, 'There will be no more delay! But in the days when the seventh angel is about to sound his trumpet, the mystery of God will be accomplished, just as He announced to His servants the prophets.'"

I believe this is the angel that I saw standing with one foot on the land and one foot on the sea in the Mediterranean and near Victor Harbor, Australia. Both places where I saw this angel were places where, historically, other gods have claimed territory.

God is releasing an arsenal of the angelic in this hour to fight back the unprecedented attempt of the enemy to gain territory. There shall be no more delay. Christ is the King of kings and Lord of lords. Even those that are lost currently in the homosexual lifestyle shall be touched by the power of God and become great evangelists and prophets, leading many to Christ. It is a declaration we must make everywhere we go.

My heart beats fast when I think of the hour that we are in. God is going to be glorified. The Church is going to rise up triumphant and shall reign in the earth by the power of Christ.

I pray that you will rise in the army of the Lord as laid down lovers whose hearts beat for God only. May you see His glory released like lightning over everyone you meet and may hope be restored to the earth once again.

CHAPTER 16

THE COMING 212 REVIVAL – THE COMING OF THE FIRE OF GOD

Confirming Signs of 212

There are times that God will speak through patterns that seem to be strange to the natural mind but He does speak in these ways nevertheless. Recently many in the prophetic movement have been noticing that God is speaking through the number "212". I myself have also experienced this number over and over in the last few months.

When I was in Australia, I did a TV interview on a show called Firestarters with my fellow prophetic minister Daryl Crawford-Marshall. As we were waiting in the lobby, waiting for Pamela Segneri to interview us, we noticed that the room number of the show was 212. It stood out to both of us as significant, even though we didn't have an understanding of what it meant at the time.

I kept seeing 212 almost the entire time I was in Australia. Sometimes these patterns can be overwhelming, especially when you don't have understanding of what they mean. When this happens to me I just begin to pray and ask God to give me revelation. He is a good Father and gives good gifts to His children and one of the best gifts is the revelation of His voice. I want to know His heart and hear Him clearly so that when He speaks I understand.

212 is a significant number for me also because my house is 212 on the street that I live. When I came back to Canada after 9 weeks in Australia, I was invited to speak at a conference in my region called "Igniting Ottawa, Awake the Nation." The meetings are taking place at 212 Murray Street in the Byward Market at the FIRE OF GOD CHURCH. The Pastor of this church is a wonderful man named Alex Ozorio who is very hungry for God do great things.

Mark Redner, one of the leaders of the Igniting Ottawa meetings and my pastor for the last 12 years, was recently in San Diego where he went to hear Jerame Nelson and Jeff Jansen preach at the San Diego Fire and Glory Outpouring. My understanding is that during the meeting Jeff asked a friend what the room number was that they were staying in and it was 212. Jeff got very excited and began to prophesy about the coming of a great revival, like the Latter Rain movement which started in New Battleford, Saskatchewan, which began on February 12, or 212.

In those meetings, Jeff also prophesied over Mark Redner and Canada declaring that "a fire would come to the country and would spread like wildfire". He said that "the tails of 300 foxes would be set on fire and that they would run through the wheat fields and fire would spread everywhere. Wheat represents the harvest and I declare the harvest will be gathered in this hour."

The Mighty Fire of God

212 is also the temperature that water begins to boil underneath the Fahrenheit scale. What is interesting to me is that most of the 212's that I mentioned above are associated with heat or fire. The TV show in Australia was called FIRESTARTERS. THE CHURCH in Ottawa where the Igniting Ottawa meetings are taking place is called the FIRE OF GOD church, and Jeff Jansen prophesied the burning of the wheat fields at the FIRE AND GLORY outpouring in San Diego, and water boils at 212.

This is suggesting to me that a mighty fire of God is coming into the Church in this hour. In fact, two days ago I was taking a nap near a beautiful lake when I had a quick vision. In this vision, I was in a waiting room in Heaven where everyone was very excited because there was coming a shift in the earth realm. Something was about to happen. I believe that this fire of God that everyone is prophesying is about to overlap the nations of the earth and many are about to be brought into the Kingdom.

We have to lay down our right to be the center of what God is doing. Many will be used to bring in this harvest. It is the way that it has always been. *Matthew 9:38* says, "**Ask the Lord of the harvest, therefore, to send out workers into His harvest field.**"

There is and always will be a need for more laborers in the harvest field. God wants to raise people up in this hour to release His fire in the earth. There will be hundreds that God will use this way. I pray that those of us who have been in ministry for a while will lay down our rights to be the center of what God is doing. God will use whoever He wants anyway.

A great revival is coming to the nations. Many would like to be the main person in the middle of what God is doing, but He chooses to be the center. He is the only center. He will move in His way and maximize the fruitfulness of every one of us. Each one of us that puts our hand to the plow in this hour will see the coming of the harvest, but we must remain humble because that is the only way we are going to see God do great things.

My prayer is that God will move in a mighty way in every town in the earth and that a harvest of souls will be brought in. My prayer is that every minister will be released from any bondage that they are under so that they can walk in a mighty way in this hour to see the gifts and fruit of the spirit released in a powerful way.

May the fire of the Holy Spirit begin to fall all around you and may your 212 season begin. Jesus is the Lord of the harvest, so as we focus on Him alone we will see great things. May His name alone be uplifted and magnified because His is the only name that can save.

CHAPTER 17

THE ISAIAH 54 ANOINTING: A TIME TO EXPAND AND TO PROSPER

Isaiah 54:2-3, "**Enlarge the place of your tent, stretch your tent curtains wide, do not hold back; lengthen your cords, strengthen your stakes. For you will spread out to the right and to the left; your descendants will dispossess nations and settle in their desolate cities**."

There are times that God speaks when there is an immediacy to what He is saying. Over the last three weeks, I have been hearing God say hundreds of times that we are in an "Isaiah 54" season. For me, this is about entering into the promises of God by force. People who will listen to what I'm saying, through this word, will be like Joshua and Caleb, who entered into the Promised Land and took that which was their inheritance in Christ Jesus our Lord.

God has more than you can even imagine for your life. Most people will live in complacency and not accept the greater blessings that God has in store for them. There is a poverty mentality in the Church in which the people of God will actually accept less than what God would have for their lives because they think they don't deserve it.

The truth is that God has more for your life than you can imagine in any one moment.

There are people reading this post right now that need some new things. There are some people who need cars, houses, boats, and planes for the Gospel's sake. **I actually believe that we are in a strong window in this moment for obtaining these things for our life.**

Jubilee, Wealth, and Inheritance

On the Jewish Calendar, we are actually in the year 5776. This is the Jewish year of Jubilee. Jubilee was instituted by God as a day when all of Israel were liberated from slavery and debt. Every 50 years God commanded that Israel returns ancestral lands to the people who became poor in the previous 50 years (*see Leviticus 25:1-4, 8-10*).

The Jews in Egypt were a people bound by slavery. When they were delivered from that life, God made it so that they would never permanently be slaves again. During the 49 years up to the Jubilee, people may have gone into debt or lost lands because of poverty; but when the Jubilee occurred they were set free and their lands were returned to them. This was an inheritance of the Lord.

Can you imagine for a moment what it must have been like for those who lived in poverty the day before Jubilee to have their lands returned to them? It was something they would never have accomplished on their own strength, but with the strength of God they became free and had their portion of wealth in Israel again.

Jubilee occurred on the day of atonement, which was the day that the High Priest went into the temple to perform the sacrifice for all of Israel. The priest would shed the blood of one lamb for the nation, but he also laid his hands on a second sacrifice and released the sin of Israel onto the head of the scapegoat. This animal was then released into the desert to live freely (*Leviticus 16*).

This very much symbolizes what Christ did for us on the Cross. There is not one of us who is without sin (Romans 3:10). There is not one of us who deserves to be free. The weight of our sin would have destroyed us if it weren't for Christ's sacrifice on the Cross.

In Christ, you and I were meant to live in Jubilee.

This is a spiritual principle about being set free from the weight and burden of sin, but I believe it is more than this. I believe Jesus intended for us to live in wealth in this world. I believe God wants us to possess the lands, to earn a good living, and to be free financially so that we are not burdened or a burden to anyone and so that we can bless many.

There are so many of you reading this that are struggling with poverty, debt, and lack. That is not a blessing. It is a curse and the people in our time are plagued with it.

Poverty is a spiritual reality that keeps people captive. It is a mentality that will keep you from entering into the promises of God for your life. Poverty will tell you that you can't obtain a greater life because you can't afford it or because you do not deserve it. Debt will lock you into failure for generations to come. Fear of finances will bind you and keep you from accomplishing great things for the Lord.

<u>Testimony of God's Faithfulness</u>

I think naturally I am what you might call a *risk taker*. In Christ, though because of the way He speaks to my heart, I have learned to take great steps of faith. This has resulted in me doing things I never imagined that I would do and obtaining things in life I have always dreamed of. In the last year, I have preached in 16 nations around the world and some of them two times.

I have driven through the rocky mountains and I have stood beside three of the earth's major oceans - the Atlantic, the Pacific, and the Indian Ocean. I have been in the Caribbean and I have been to the Mediterranean sea.

At the beginning of this year, I had so much debt and my car was really old. I needed a new car, but in the natural, I would have had to wait three more years to get it. Well, today I have new cars. I know that many get upset when we begin to talk about possessing material things, but God is not upset about this. I have learned to give these things away when God tells me to. I have given two vehicles away this year, plus some of my salary.

When God says that He is going to expand you, and really this is what Isaiah 54 is about, there is nothing that you have to fear. When the 12 spies went into the Canaan land and saw the giants, they were terrified. However, God actually would have destroyed those giants if they had stepped into believing that He could. As a result, they spent 40 years in the desert wandering until a generation rose up that could believe that God would help them with their giants.

Who are the people in this generation that will believe for more? I intend to be one of those. I grew up in a relatively poverty culture where I lived. As a young man, I asked the Lord for wisdom to help me to enter a better life for myself. He has helped me all along the way.

Every step that I have taken has been by faith. Everything that I have has come when I dared to believe that God has more for my life. I got my house this way, I got my education this way, and my small business and ministry have grown as a result of listening to Him. He has more for you than you are even willing to receive.

I challenge you today to believe for more. I pray that God gives you the faith to enter into His greatest promises yet. Get ready for your Isaiah 54 season. Get ready for your Jubilee. Get ready to be a sign and a wonder to the nations of the great provision that God provides to His people.

CHAPTER 18

GOD'S GLORY IS GOING TO OVERWHELM AND HEAL YOU

Over the last few days, I have been hearing God say that He is about to tear the walls down in our lives that keep us bound in anxiety and fear. I have been hearing that He is about to accelerate this healing so that people will be prepared for the blessings that He has for them in the next season. This is a good reason to receive healing from the Lord.

A few days ago, I heard the Lord say that He is about to release the "Guided Glory Missiles" which will enter into the deepest places of resistance in our hearts. These are areas of our lives where we have been struggling emotionally for a long time. Some of the people that are about to receive His healing will even have clinical definitions given to them by the medical community and some of them will seem incurable in the natural.

These glory bombs are going to overwhelm you with the love of God. You are going to see life differently. I remember about five years ago I had such a deliverance in my life that the very next day I saw colors differently. I was driving down a highway and couldn't drive the car fast because all I wanted to do was look at the colors of God's creation. I had never experienced a moment like that before.

My Personal Deliverance

God is able to deliver us from anything. When I first came to Christ 12 years ago, I was suffering with suicidal thoughts and with severe depression. I had feared so deep in my heart that I use to sleep on my mother's floor because I didn't want to sleep in my room alone; I was so afraid. I was 32 years of age. I wonder how many of us would be this honest. It makes me laugh now to see how far I have come. I couldn't even sleep with the lights off back then.

My testimony is that God showed up in dreams and visions and began to heal me of many of the things that held me captive in my life. When He began to speak to me I understood that He was the Creator of the universe, and I had nothing to fear.

His healing never stops. He is constantly dealing with the pains of my heart, and I am constantly receiving His grace day by day. This is what I believe is the renewal of the mind that the Apostle Paul spoke about.

Romans 12:2 says, "**Do not conform to the pattern of this world, but be transformed by the renewing of your mind. Then you will be able to test and approve what God's will is--His good, pleasing and perfect will.**"

2 Corinthians 3:18 says, "**And we all, who with unveiled faces contemplate the Lord's glory, are being transformed into His image with ever-increasing glory, which comes from the Lord, who is the Spirit**."

When we pass the place of the flesh and enter beyond the veil into life in the spirit, our emotions come to peace. What we need is the Holy Spirit to draw us deeper and deeper into the place of God's thoughts for our lives. When His thoughts overwhelm us we become new because they help form a new identity inside of us. This identity is from God and not from satan or man. It is an identity that helps us to truly function in the earth.

Walls Are Coming Down...Chains Are Being Broken

Yesterday I heard the Lord say that "The walls are coming down in people's lives," and He likened it to the walls of Jericho. He said that the enemy has strongholds in our lives that seem impenetrable but they are about to come down. These are areas of hurt that people have been living with for a long time. When God's Word comes to you like a flood, you are going to be overwhelmed by His goodness and peace will enter into the places of brokenness in your life.

The enemy will be silenced by the goodness of our Lord. You don't have to worry because this is not something you can do by your own strength or power. This is something that God is going to do as a sign and wonder of His great love for you. What He does for your life will also

become a possibility for many other lives. Your life is going to become a prophetic expression of the goodness of God. God wants to set every single person free. When He moves in your life He is saying that He can move in every life.

The key for your life is to seek God with all your heart. The promise from God is that if you seek Him you will find Him if you seek Him with all your heart (Jeremiah 29:13); and that which you seek is going to be more valuable than money can buy. It is the pearl of great price (*Matthew 13:45-46*).

It is worth leaving all behind because that which Jesus has prepared for you is greater than anything you can ever imagine.

My hope and my prayer for you is that you will find Christ in the center of your heart. Even now I see people with chains holding them down. Christ is standing beside you with a hammer that can destroy those chains. Just call out to Him and He is faithful and will change your every circumstance.

Father, open up the floodgates and release a million thoughts of good into the people's lives. Let them know that You love them and care for them and have a plan for them.

Call Unto Him

Jeremiah 33:3 says, "**Call to Me, and I will answer you, and show you great and mighty things, which you do not know**." This is not just a passage in the Bible it is a promise and it is for you.

When I first got this passage I woke up two nights in a row and on the clock it was 3:33 am. I knew that God was saying something but wasn't sure what. A few days later I heard a preacher preach from this passage. I knew that it was God's great joy to give me revelation for my life to bring healing and deliverance. And it is His joy to do the same for you. You are about to reccive revelation that will set you free.

So seek Him and you will find Him. Press into His heart and He will press toward you and great healing will come to you like a flood. Your mind will be overwhelmed by His "Glory Missiles" that are coming your way and you will walk and not grow weary and run and not faint.

CHAPTER 19

GOD'S HEALING MANIFESTED: EIGHT STEPS TO CLAIM HIS HEALING FOR YOU

Here are eight steps to claim His healing over you. Be greatly blessed and encouraged:

1. Knowing That God is More Powerful Than the Health Crisis You Face

Isaiah 41:10 **"So do not fear, for I am with you; do not be dismayed, for I am your God. I will strengthen you and help you; I will uphold you with My righteous right hand.** *"*

The truth is we all fear at times. This is not God's best for our lives; but unless we know God completely, we walk in uncertainty when we face new situations and trials.

Until we have the witness that God heals, we do not know He heals. You may know on an intellectual level that God is the Healer, but until you have experienced Him as the

Healer you may not have the certainty that He will heal you. When you experience healing and see God's hand move upon your life, your faith is strengthened. So pray that God will heal you so that your faith increases for more healing.

2. Having Faith in God

Hebrews 11:6 says, **"But without faith, it is impossible to please Him, for he who comes to God must believe that He is and that He is a rewarder of those who diligently seek Him.** *"*

Your faith may seem small in your own eyes but it doesn't take much. An action like stepping out to go to a place to receive prayer, or allowing yourself to be anointed with oil, or doing the Lord's supper could be all that it takes for you to be healed.

Your natural mind may not understand God, but as you speak to yourself and as you confess your faith even despite your circumstances God will move. When you go deep into the things of the Holy Spirit and as you continue to walk with Him, you will begin to understand that it is impossible for God not to do what His Word says He will do.

There have been plenty of times when I have faced health issues that don't seem to be getting better, but I have always continued to believe despite my situation. God is still the God that heals me of all my diseases (see Psalm 103:3) even if I have not seen the healing in the moment. **I will continue to believe He is the Healer until my situation changes.**

3. Healing is Part of the Blessing of God

Exodus 15:26 says, **"If you diligently heed the voice of the Lord your God and do what is right in His sight, give ear to His commandments and keep all His statutes, I will put none of the diseases on you which I have brought on the Egyptians. For I am the Lord who heals you.***"*

One of the many blessings of God is that you will walk in good health. It is actually one of the blessings that was promised to Israel when they came into covenant with God, as outlined in the Scripture above. As long as they did what was right then they would be healed and they would not experience ill health.

When you begin to understand the power of God's covenant then you begin to know that when sickness does come it is not God's will.

I often find myself saying to God, **"Lord I am Your son and I do my best try to obey You, however, if there is an area of my life that is not submitted then please help me and change me***.*"

I do this because I don't want there to be one area in my life where I have a hole where satan can sneak in to steal, kill and destroy. **I want abundant life and that only comes through Christ. As I repent and as I come out of agreement with the enemy's lies over my life through the power of God's Word, I am made whole.**

The blessing of God comes on my life because of Christ. When I actually understand the Word of God and the covenant of His many blessings, I am in a better place to receive His gift of healing. So continue reading His Word, looking for His promises so that you know what is yours in Christ Jesus.

4. Knowing That Christ Died on the Cross For All Your Diseases

Isaiah 53:5 says, *"***But He was pierced for our transgressions, He was crushed for our iniquities; the punishment that brought us peace was on Him, and by His wounds, we are healed***."*

If you truly digest this Scripture you will see something terrific and powerful within it. **Healing is a foundation of the new covenant.** When man was outside of Christ and under the power of the curse, sickness and disease were anathemas that kept us down, but in Christ, we are healed.

It is a part of the covenant, a part of Christ's sacrifice. It is in the atonement. Just as we are forgiven of our sins, so by His stripes we are healed. There is no disease that is not covered by this promise. Once this truth starts to hit your heart, the hope that is within it is amazing. You can continue to believe even when it doesn't look good because God still has to heal.

There are times that I have carried His promise many days and months before the manifestation of my healing has come, but in the end, I have always received my healing because I know He has to heal me.

5. Prayer is Always Key

My faith is not as important as the strength of my God. I may be weak but He is strong. If my faith is small I usually pray and ask God to strengthen it so that I will believe for more. In this way, I am much like the man that said to Jesus, **"I believe but help me with my unbelief"** (*Mark 9:24*).

God knows who you are. He knows what you believe and what you don't believe. You may have strong faith that God can provide for your needs according to His riches in glory, but perhaps you are not sure if He can give you a new heart or not. Well, just pray continuously. Thank God for all your trials but also thank Him for teaching you all things. Thank Him for revealing Himself. Thank Him for strengthening your faith in your trial.

However, if you don't believe, tell Him. Ask the Holy Spirit to reveal God as your Healer and He will. As you pray this way your understanding of God will inevitably be strengthened. You will grow as you are honest with Him.

6.) Getting a Vision For Your Health Outcome

One of the foundations of my faith is that God is a good God and He speaks to us in many ways. I often pray and ask God what He is going to do with my life, including my health. In fact, I have often asked Him for a dream or a vision to show me what He wanted to do. When He does show me, I know that I have what He has revealed because He cannot lie.

One time, the Lord showed me my youngest son as a 10-month-old baby sitting on the floor healthy and having a good time. Within a few weeks of this vision, and shortly after he was born, he stopped breathing and turned blue. He seemed to have died. When I found out that he was in this condition, I told my wife to remember what the Lord had shown us as this became strength for us. It helped the both of us to get to the outcome. In fact, he made it through this situation very well and today is a healthy young boy, the biggest of all his brothers.

Acts 2 speaks of a Church that is filled with the Holy Spirit and one that will walk in dreams and visions. Declare this even over your own life and then begin to ask God to show you all things pertaining to your own life including how He intends to heal you and your loved ones.

7. Healing is a Sign That Follows the Gospel

Jesus said to His disciples in *Mark 16:17-18*, "**And these signs shall follow them that believe; In My Name shall they cast out devils; they shall speak with new tongues; They shall take up serpents; and if they drink any deadly thing, it shall not hurt them; they shall lay hands on the sick, and they shall recover**."

This is a promise that Jesus made. **Given the authority from which He said it as the risen Savior, my expectation** is that what He said will come to pass. As I continue to preach and declare Jesus Christ as Lord, healing is a sign that will follow my life. Not only will I be healed but the many people I pray for will also be healed. **This is my expectation and my reality and a promise from my risen Savior.**

8. Be Persistent in Asking

The widow in Jesus' parable in *Luke 18:1-8* continued to ask the Judge for help. The judge himself said, *"**Though I do not fear God nor regard man, yet because this widow troubles me I will avenge her, lest by her continual coming she weary me**" (v 4-5).*

I consider myself to be the persistent widow. I will not stop, day or night, asking God to help me, to guide me, to deliver me and to heal me. I know He is a good Father and that He delights in giving good gifts to His children.

A gentile woman came to Jesus asking Him to heal her daughter. Because she was a gentile and not Jewish Jesus said to her in *Matthew 15:26*, *"**'First let the children eat all they want,' He told her, 'for it is not right to take the children's bread and toss it to the dogs.'**"* In this instance, He is referring to the Jews as the children and all other people as dogs. Under the old covenant, this made complete sense.

Jesus was the Messiah of the Jews and He was there for their healing, but the woman recognized a deeper truth and responded by saying, *"'Lord,' she replied, 'even the dogs under the table eat the children's crumbs'" (v 27)*. As a result of this statement, the child was healed.

Continue praying and continue seeking for God to manifest Himself as your Healer and you will experience your healing. The truth of healing will be witnessed in your life as you continue to push into God.

CHAPTER 20

GOD IS RAISING UP THE PILLARS OF THE EARTH

About a month ago, I had a dream in which I was standing in a high place looking down at the earth. I was amazed at what I saw. It was as if all the soil of the earth was removed so that I could see what laid underneath; and there, in the middle of the earth, there were these giant pillars.

The pillars or columns that I saw were much like the columns used in Roman and Greek architecture, or what you might see at the White House. They were huge and imposing. They were greater in size than any skyscraper I had ever seen, and entire towns and cities could rest upon the top of them.

There wasn't just one of these columns but there were many. Each together were holding the earth in its place.

What's The Interpretation of the Dream?

When I saw this, I really had no idea what it was I was seeing. I knew that it was significant but didn't have the interpretation of my dream. What I love about the Body of Christ is that we are knitted together because God desires that we depend on each other. When I don't have understanding of my dreams, I usually call people to help me interpret them. In this case, I called my mother. My mother is an amazing woman of God who has a great way of interpreting dreams, but in this instance, she had very little understanding of the dream.

As I was talking to my mother on my phone, my wife was sitting at the kitchen table. She was trying to get my attention as she was pointing at her own phone. I knew she had something she wanted to say but I was concentrating on the call with my mother. (Yes, I know that I just got in a lot of trouble with wives everywhere...if I could insert a smiley face here, laughing at myself, I would.)

My wife had the interpretation of the dream. She looked at me and said, **"Your dream is much like this Scripture that I am reading in** *1 Samuel 2:8*, **which states,**

'He raises the poor from the dust
And lifts the beggar from the ash heap,
To set them among princes
And make them inherit the throne of glory.
'For the pillars of the earth are the Lord's,
And He has set the world upon them.'"

Rescued from the Ash Heaps

This Scripture is really a prophetic picture of you and me in Christ. Not many of us were nobles or rich when Christ found us. Perhaps, you were like me. When Christ found me

I was in the middle of a suicide attempt. I was an atheist who didn't believe that God could speak and I was very sinful. I was both relieved and filled with terror when I heard God speak to me that day.

I did not believe there was an afterlife. I thought that if I killed myself, I would sink back into the black abyss from which I imagined I came; but now that God was speaking to me, I began to fathom eternity much differently than what I had conjured in my own mind. Perhaps there were consequences I would have to deal with if I killed myself after all.

He literally rescued me from the ash heap. In other interpretations of this Scripture, you will see the word "Dung Hill." I think we can all agree that this is not a good place to exist. It is a place where you find people in the worst possible conditions. **They are broken and filled with every sordid sin and yet God takes them and places them in seats of honor.** God doesn't need our permission to do this either.

In Christ, We Are The Pillars of the Earth

You and I in Christ can become these pillars. We can become strength for many. A person who is established and rooted in Christ has the ability to shed abroad the love of Jesus to many hearts. **The key is to remain in God's voice and to be washed in His presence. You must allow Jesus to transform your life from the inside out.**

Hebrews 11:8 says that **"By faith Abraham, when called to go to a place he would later receive as his inheritance, obeyed and went, even though he did not know where he**

was going. *"* This act of faith separated Abraham from his generation and helped him to enter into the promises that God had for him. Not many people would do what he did, but those that will obey God will become strength for many generations to come.

Characteristics of the Pillars

When I think of pillars, I think of my grandparents, who believed in God and followed Him fearlessly. They used to tell me when I was young that they prayed for me every day and I know that they did. In their generation, they were faithful, and as a result, they strengthened the generations to come. **My desire is to become the same strength to my family for generations to come. My prayer is that my offspring will be found faithful because I was faithful.**

The pillars are men and women of God who stand up in hours of great darkness and become great lights in their times. I think of John Wesley, who brought great revival to England and to America. The times that he lived in were as dark as the times in which we live. In fact, when he started to minister, they say there were only 4 or 5 members of Parliament in England that were actually Christian, but this man of God was faithful in his generation and affected great change in the culture of his time.

Wesley had to resort to preaching in open fields because the Anglican Church would not receive him. When I was in Sheffield, England I learned that 15,000 or 1/3 of the city showed up to hear him preach in an open field. He was ridiculed, ignored and even persecuted by many, and yet today there are over 30 million people that still associate themselves to the Wesleyan or Methodist Church worldwide. **I don't imagine that in his lifetime, he would have thought this would happen, and yet it did. He became a pillar of the earth in his generation and in the generations to come.**

I believe that God is raising up people like Wesley in this generation. There is a call and an invitation to be faithful. **I believe that God showed me these pillars in my dream to declare that our generation will also be faithful in Christ and we will become known as a generation that put God above all things**.

In your heart today, determine that you will become that pillar and I believe you will. I pray that God strengthens you and empowers you to become the light of Christ to those around you inspiring them to great faithfulness.

CHAPTER 21

ABUNDANCE! WE'RE IN A SEASON OF INCREASE AND PLENTY

<u>Great Expectations This Year!</u>

Over the years I have seen the glory train many times, but recently I saw it again. I had dream in early December that there were new tracks in my city, and there was a new train running through it. It was a train that was characteristic of my city but it was new. The fare was quite cheap, but there were some who were not able to pay. I asked the conductor where the train was headed, and he told me *down to Riverside*. So I am expecting to see God move in incredible ways again this year. Something new is going to begin and it is going to be remembered. What will occur will become foundational for the next twenty years.

My city of Ottawa is building a New Light Rail Train System which is to be completed this year in celebration of Canada's 150th anniversary. Stage 2 of the project begins in 2018. I just learned recently (about month after I had this dream) that one of the planned lines will end in Riverside (an Ottawa neighborhood). God is speaking, but who is listening? Get ready for a new level of glory to come to the Church!

Financial Blessings - Get Ready for God to Bless You!

This year, God is going to download strategies into His people that will increase them financially. Pay attention to your gut instincts, or your sixth sense. The Lord is going to speak by the Holy Spirit and words of knowledge. Those people who are listening are going to hear things that if they will follow through on, will prosper them in incredible ways.

I see people even getting wealthy through the Stock Market this year. When this revelation came to me, I got very excited because God is about to bring the money of the nations into the hands of Christians. Christians will be known as wise and understanding when it comes to the ways of money.

I feel that there are some who are about to experience deliverance from spirits that are holding them back from financial blessing. I saw an amazing house in my dream. The first time I saw it, there was a man living there all alone. I noticed a picture of him on the wall, where there was an aggressive figure hovering over him. This was a generational spirit that oppressed him and kept blessing from flowing into him.

Then I saw the house again, but this time it was filled with great blessing and the aggressive spirit was gone, and so was the picture! Your deliverance time is here! Get ready for God to bless you in new ways! Get ready for increase. Get ready for your house to be filled with new glory because the enemy can no longer hold you.

Yet, in order to enter into the things that God has for you in this next season, God will begin to do heart surgery on your life. Some of us are going to feel very heavy in the initial phases of this new change, like a patient receiving anesthetic. You may even feel like a heaviness is coming over you because of the changes that are taking place in your life.

Let God do His work in you and watch the changes that will start coming by June and July. Some of you will be living in situations next autumn that you never imagined you would be living in. Great favor and prosperity will be coming to you. But you will have to access this by faith. Some of the things that God wants to give you are so great, that this will result in you having to be completely changed in your mindset in order to step into it.

Market Place Miracles and Mantles

God is about to move in the marketplace by miracles, signs, and wonders. I saw this in a dream where miracles were taking place in coffee shops. Gold dust was appearing in abundance on people's hands. As they saw these signs and wonders, it actually opened up the people to receive prayer in Jesus' name. We also began to see people healed of all kinds of sicknesses and diseases! I declare that this is the season of many coming to Christ supernaturally.

God is releasing this month new mantles. I had a DREAM where I was in a shoe store in Heaven and I saw dozens of pairs of glorious heaven-made shoes. There were shoes there that were absolutely stunning and available for those who are willing to pay the price. You will receive God's power within you to achieve God's destiny for your life. As you seek Him in this season I believe that God is about to release *new thought patterns* to you to enter into greater fulfillment and destiny. He wants to bless you and use you for His glory.

My prayer for you today is that everything that God has in store for your life will come to pass. I pray that every obstacle, every attack of the enemy will cease so that you will soar like the eagle. I see God destroying the effect that time has had on your life. Things in this season are going to accelerate. You will accomplish things very quickly. What would have been normal over four years you will now accomplish in one. You are going to get a return on the time that was stolen from you by the enemy.

ABOUT THE AUTHOR

A Voice to the Nations

Darren Canning is a preacher, writer, artist, father, and husband. He has traveled widely releasing God's words of destiny over lives, towns, and regions. He has been to 18 nations and operates with a strong prophetic and healing gift and sees many people touched by the power of God.

Darren is a regular contributor to many prophetic publications including the Elijah List, Spirit-Fuel, and the Identity Network. His writings have been read worldwide by hundreds of thousands of people. He has a passion to reach people through social media. He has been interviewed by the Trinity Broadcasting Network, Firestarters TV, Radio Air Jesus and a few other TV programs.

Darren came out of a life of agnosticism and once worked for the Canadian Government as an Economic Analyst. He is now full time in ministry and travels the nations releasing his message of hope.

Dear Reader,

If your life was touched while reading this book please let us know! We would love to celebrate with you! Please visit our website www.darrencanning.com for contact information.

May God bless you and keep you,

Darren Canning

For More books by Darren Canning search for him on Amazon and Kindle!

"A presence-driven publisher making your book
dream come true!"

www.deeperlifepress.com
www.findrefuge.tv

For more info on Darren Canning's ministry see our website
www.darrencanning.com
Contact Info
Darren Canning Ministries
212 Franktown Road
Carleton Place, Ontario
K7C 2N7
www.darrencanning.com

Manufactured by Amazon.ca
Bolton, ON